The God-Shaped Hole

Veronica Brady

The God-Shaped Hole:

Responding to the Good News in Australia

Veronica Brady

ATF Press
Adelaide

Text copyright © 2008 remains with Veronica Brady.

All rights reserved. Except for any fair dealing permitted under the Copyright Act, no part of this book may be reproduced by any means without prior permission. Inquiries should be made to the publisher.

Cover design by Astrid Sengkey

ATF Press
An imprint of the Australasian Theological Forum Ltd
P O Box 504
Hindmarsh
SA 5007
ABN 90 116 359 963
www.atfpress.com

Contents

Preface		ix
1.	'God Is Dead, Anyway. Anyway—Thank God—In Australia.'	1
2.	'Keep Your Mind In Hell And Despair Not.' For *The Term of His Natural Life* And The Possibilities Of Isolation	9
3.	Human Distress And Suffering: The Question Of The Holocaust. Primo Levi's *If This Is A Man*	21
4.	The Dragon Slayer: Patrick White And History	33
5.	Borders, Identity And Australia	41
6.	The Poetics Of Place: Judith Wright's 'At Cooloola'	51
7.	An Incident In The Culture Wars: Judith Wright's 'Haunted Land'	61
8.	Blasphemy And Sacrilege In The Arts: The Challenge Of Kim Scott's *Benang*	71
9.	After Cronulla: The Defense Of *The White Earth*	81
10.	'Are We Here But To Name The World?': Ways Of Naming And Praising	89
11.	An Apology For The Library And For 'The Golden World Of The Imagination': A Neo-Luddite View	97

12. 'What Is Truth?', Said Jesting Pilate, And Did Not Stay
    To Hear   111

13. 'Such Is Life My Fellow Mummers':
    The Seditious Joseph Furphy   117

Preface

From childhood I have had a sense that (as Job finally realized), we are surrounded by 'what [we] do not understand, things too wonderful for [us] . . . which [we] do not know.' Not, of course, that my life has been anything like Job's. I have not come to this understanding through suffering. Indeed I have managed to sail happily through life, gifted with loving parents, family and friends and, as a 'religious', with a generously understanding and caring community, given every opportunity to develop whatever talents I may possess. But it is possible, I think, to learn through happiness as well as pain. Pain often seems to destroy the sense of wonder Job spoke of, turning it into anger and fear. Perhaps more importantly, happiness can generate the belief that some ultimate, if mysterious, good exists and can be trusted. With that belief even in the midst of suffering, hope is able to survive—as one of my essays suggests.

So for most of my life I have been trying to explore the mystery of 'realities at present unseen' (as the New Teastament *Letter To the Hebrews* defines faith—a word which seems to me a better word than 'religion' which can often become either a 'cosmic Linus blanket' or a declaration of superiority.) This preoccupation, I suspect, has made me an odd kind of academic—at least in the humanities—since it means that I tend to stray from its accepted notions of reality. Nevertheless I take comfort from the direction in which the contemporary sciences seem to be moving which seems to be in a more 'poetic' direction. The physicist John Polkinghorne, for instance, speculates that the universe may be 'more open, more subtle, and more supple in its character' and thus more difficult to understand than commonsense has allowed.

At the same time my views—though explorations might be a better description—have also troubled some religious people; indeed in some quarters they have been seen as heretical, threatening true and traditional belief. But as I see it whatever the word 'God' points to is necessarily beyond our comprehension and, as Dietrich Bonhoeffer wrote in his *Letters and Papers From Prison*, should not be used 'as a stop-gap for the incompleteness of our knowledge'. As he says, we must accept that incompleteness and get ourselves out of 'the one-track' approach to reality our culture imposes on us by recognising and accepting that existence is not monotone but polyphonic and therefore that, 'God wants us to love him eternally with all our hearts—not in such a way as to injure or weaken our earthly love, but to provide a kind of *cantus firmus* to which the other melodies of life provide the counterpoint'. That means, I think, we should be deeply and lovingly involved in the world in which we live, but should also acknowledge that, as Cardinal Newman noted, to live is to change and to grow is to change often, so that tradition is dynamic not static.

It also presupposes that the God in whom we believe—or, as one of Patrick White's characters, the 'dill' Arthur Brown in *The Solid Mandala*, puts it, believes in us—is to be found not only in special set apart 'sacred' places, people and situations but in the midst of everyday life with all its complicated ambiguities. As contemporary theologian Eberhard Jüngel expresses it, in his *God as the Mystery of the World*: God 'goes on ways to God-self through this world', even, he says, through places which may not seem godly. For that reason, as Bonhoeffer suggested, today we may need to speak of God in a 'secular' way, without religious language, concentrating instead on finding where God may be meeting us in our particular place and time, in a 'God-shaped hole' in our experience.

Preface

This is the area I have been trying to mine in these essays, not to downgrade the importance of theology, however, but to increase its range and significance. It also, I hope, helps us to confront the challenge posed by thinkers like Marx, Nietzsche and Freud for whom 'God' was merely a projection of psychological, social and even economic cowardice. We are concerned here with experiencing a hole, an interruption, even a wound though it may also be an experience of joy and an intuition of what Nietzsche called the 'transvaluation of value'.

Conventional theological writing finds it difficult to deal with this kind of experience which seems to me central to the experience of the God. This Gods revealed himself/herself to Moses in the burning bush which was never consumed and in the voice proclaiming 'I AM WHO I AM'; it has also been translated as 'I AM WHO I WILL BE FOR YOU'. But the arts, literature especially, may bring us closer than theology since they work through symbols, expressing what Patrick White, to refer to him again, referred to as 'what you do not know but *know*' and thus liberates us from the one-dimensional rationality which imprisons so many of us today.

Don Quixote has always been one of my heroes, living out seemingly impossible dreams in a matter-of-fact world. He lived in sixteenth century Spain, of course, whereas I live in Australia, a new society only two hundred years old, intent on material reality. But it is also an ancient land which has been inhabited for thousands of years by peoples whose culture is the oldest living one in the world. So we have still to explore this other culture and the suffering and sorrow we have inflicted on its peoples (but also in the process on ourselves). Only then will we be able to make this land the place of a new beginning, a new world, a place of the Spirit.

That probably sounds foolishly romantic. But it is the possibility I have been trying to explore, believing that the first step in this direction is to expand our sense of reality, to recognize that, as William Blake insisted, a line 'is not merely up and down', that we need to redefine what we mean by reality and value and accept that there are 'more things in heaven and earth' than are contemplated by our commonsense so that our human reason is not the measure of all reality—as thinkers like Richard Dawkins insist.

These essays—a collection of papers given in different places over the last few years[1]—I hope, are pointing towards a deeper sense of the mystery of things and of the responsibility it imposes on us to and for others and the world around us since, as Emmanuel Levinas argues, it is 'in the laying down by the ego of its sovereignty (in its hateful modality), that we find ethics and also probably the spirituality of the soul . . . and the meaning of being.'

The reader will note that there are a number of constant dialogue partners: poets, literary critics, philosophers and theologians (Wright, White, Ricoeur, Eliade, Levinas, Metz, and Jüngel to name a few). These companions on the way are those with whom my different approaches to poetry, literary, philosophy and theology find resonance.

I am grateful for the work that both Alan Cadwallader and Hilary Regan of ATF Press have put into this work. They have produced a monograph of essays from a bunch of papers I have given over the last few years in different places. Thank you.

Let me conclude then on an enigmatic note by quoting one of Emily Dickinson's untitled poems in which she reflects on this meaning of being—with the reminder that

---

1. All the essays in this collection were written before the change of government in Australia in November 2007. Editorial changes have been made throughout.

Preface

the 'bark' (sailing ship) is a traditional symbol of human existence surrounded as it is by 'what we do not know but *know*'.

> Whether my bark went down at sea,
> Whether she met with gales,
> Whether to isles enchanted
> She bent her docile sails;
>
> By what mystic mooring
> She is held today,—
> This is the errand of the eye
> Out upon the bay.

Veronica Brady
Perth, Western Australia
January 2008

1

'God Is Dead, Anyway. Anyway—Thank God—In Australia.'

The quotation with which we begin, from Patrick White's *The Vivisector*, points to the paradox I want to explore: the ways in which God, 'the unacknowledged factor', may continue to work in a secular society like Australia, a society in which, as the quotation suggests, God is largely disregarded. The conversation which provides my title is between two fashionable people at a retrospective exhibition of the work of White's fictional painter, Hurtle Duffield, and their opinions are typical enough. But if we accept the importance of symbolic expression for deciphering what may be otherwise inexpressible in a secular culture like ours, it is worth reflecting on the fact that the life of Duffield, the novel's protagonist, turns on his attempt to 'paint God', 'the otherwise unnameable I-N-D-I-G-O' (White, 1970: 641)—indigo being the ultimate colour in the alchemical spectrum. Duffield dies in a final attempt to do so. The novel thus suggests not only that, as this conversation implies, the word itself means little or nothing to many perhaps most Australians, but also that what it actually refers to is beyond words, as Jean-Luc Marion puts it, *'hors-texte'* ('without being') (Marion, 1991). And yet it is so important that it is worth dying for.

I want to begin by arguing, paradoxically perhaps, that the apparent disbelief in God may not be as negative as it sounds, at least if we accept that religion, which the Macquarie Dictionary defines as a 'a particular system in which the quest for the ideal life has been embodied', is not necessarily the same as faith, a personal 'commitment to realities at present unseen' (*Hebrews* 11:1). Many cultures, however, tend to see the two as synonymous, which often means that religion replaces faith. As Marx —following Feuerbach—pointed out, what many people call God is a projection of emotional, social, economic or political need (Easton and Guddat, 1967: 250). So the fact that our culture is officially secular may leave more room for the living God, the God beyond words, whose best definition, as JB Metz suggests, may be 'interruption'. But before we go any further, we need to reflect on the kind of society in which we find ourselves.

It is a settler society, one in which, in contrast to traditional societies, the self's primary question tends to be 'what world can I possess?' rather than 'where do I belong in the scheme of things?' Ours is also the product of British imperial history which tended to be less concerned than the earlier empires of Spain and Portugal with spreading the gospel than with economics and politics, specifically in our case with relieving the pressure on Britain's overcrowded prisons and with establishing a base for trade in the Pacific. For these reasons, our beginnings were not particularly gracious. The arrival of the First Fleet was less monumental than orgiastic, and, for some time, might was often more important than right—indeed, some would suggest that this is still the case.

In this situation, the civil religion the Establishment brought with them functioned as a more or less optional extra while for the Irish, many of them convicts or struggling settlers, the Holy Roman Empire represented their answer to the British Empire. But this could be seen as an opportunity for the God who exists outside the text of history, though he/she also intervenes in it. As Ian Turner observed:

> A religion which was appropriate for the ordered society and regular living of rural England seemed irrelevant to pioneering labour in the Australian bush. Men carved their own lives out of a remote and monstrously difficult wilderness; what they achieved they owed to themselves, and they found little for which to thank their fathers' heaven (Turner, 1968: x).

Nevertheless for those of us who believe in the God whose 'being is in coming . . . [who] goes on ways to himself, even when they lead to other places, even to that which is not God', ways which can 'include something like distance from himself too' (Jüngel, 1983: 159), what someone has called a 'God-shaped hole', must exist even here.

This hole is often apparent in literature and the arts generally. So let us return to Patrick White, to a passage from another novel, *The Solid Mandala*. The conversation this time is between Arthur Brown, a young man who is seen especially by his intellectually pretentious twin brother as a 'dill'. His pious but well-meaning neighbour Mrs Poulter asks Arthur why none of his family ever went to church, to which he replies that they 'began to feel it wasn't true'. This shocks her and she tells him that she 'couldn't exist without Our Lord'. His response, however, echoes Marx's critique of mere religion, asking: 'Could He exist without *you*?' Arthur has no time for pious statements, knowing from experience that many 'Christians are cruel', ready to 'crucify' people like him who are different (White, 1966: 261–2). Later, however, he dances out for her his vision of God as the crucified one, involved in our pain. Eventually, after Arthur's death, Mrs Poulter understands what he has been saying, when she catches a glimpse of the sufferings of the wars and violence of our times as the 'God' of her complacencies falls 'down, in a thwack of canvas, a cloud of dust' (White, 1961: 303). This theme runs like a refrain through White's work: 'Man is not God' contrary to what 'our fevers for power' make us think, but also shows himself often as 'Man with a spear in his side' (White, 1971: 296–7).

This suggests that the suspicion of organised religion, apparent in our culture, though somewhat diminished today by the growth of fundamentalism, may have theological significance. One of the founding figures of the 'Australian tradition' in our literature, Joseph Furphy, for instance, rejected what he called 'phylactered exclusivism', seeing 'ecclesiastical Christianity . . . as a failure of the first magnitude'. For Furphy, it had made the cross, 'the symbol of deepest ignominy . . . the proudest insignia of court-moths and professional assassins' (Barnes, 1981: 89–90). For him, God 'is by his own authority represented by the poorest of the poor' (Barnes, 1981: 86). In this respect, the tradition of the 'fair go', the belief that, in the words of seventeenth century Christian John Lilburne, 'the poorest he hath as much right as the richest he and demands our respect and care', has religious significance.

Yet it does not really address what I see as the central question which is both ontological and epistemological, the question of authority: whether or not there is a reality beyond human history to which we owe obedience. By definition, as we have said, our society is the product of imperial history, but a history which was, in the nineteenth century, fuelled by the neo-Darwinism which replaced belief in God with belief in historical inevitability, in the evolutionary struggle of all against all in which the fittest—people like us—were destined to triumph. It made the imperial self 'the basis and referent of the whole of reality spread out at its feet' (Susin, 2000: 80), locking us in a 'closed circle around sameness' (Susin,

2000: 87), with disastrous consequences for the land's First Peoples but also for the land and its flora and fauna.

If we return to the belief that God continues to go on ways to God-self through this world and also that this God may manifest himself as the crucified, however, it appears that God may be speaking to us in these wounded ones, calling us out of our closed circle to recognise the claims of the other/Other upon us. This is our crucial opportunity since, as Emmanuel Levinas argues, it 'is in the laying down by the ego of its sovereignty [in this way] . . . that we find ethics and also probably the very spirituality of the soul, but most certainly the question of the meaning of being' (Hand, 1993: 85). The recognition that the environmental crisis is urging on us, is challenging the arrogance of our exploitative culture in this way. But for the moment let us conclude with a brief reflection on the significance for us of Aboriginal Australia.

The biblical figure of the Suffering Servant, I suggest, is important here. 'Despised and rejected by others; a man of suffering acquainted with infirmity' who has in fact been 'wounded for our transgressions, crushed for our iniquities'; this figure is nevertheless the one 'through whom the will of the Lord shall prosper' (*Isaiah*, 55: 3, 5, 10). This, I suggest, is because, in contemplating his fate, we may understand who we really are before God but also what we must do if we are to realise God's will for us. It thus calls us to renounce our allegiance to the dynamisms of contemporary history and give our allegiance to God's logic according to which the true meaning of human history may lie with the 'losers' rather than the 'winners'. As Walter Benjamin puts it: 'Victory bears its fruits entirely differently from the way in which defeat has its consequences' (Mertens, 2006: 76).

These fruits are theological. Although they are at a discount in a secular age, it is our task to accept that this is so and to live out the consequences. In the long run, I would argue, it is they which will enable us to survive.

References

Barnes, John, editor, *Portable Australian Authors: Joseph Furphy* (St Lucia: University of Queensland Press, 1981).

Easton, Lloyd and Guddat, Kurt, editors, *Writings Of The Young Marx On Philosophy And Society* (New York: Doubleday Anchor Book, 1967).

Hand, Sean, editor, *The Levinas Reader* (Oxford: Blackwell, 1993).

Jüngel, Eberhard, *God As The Mystery Of The World*, translated by Darrell Guder (Grand Rapids: Eerdman, 1983).

Marion, Jean-Luc, *God Without Being* (London: University of Chicago Press, 1991).

Mertens, Bram, 'Benjamin: 'Hope, Yes, But Not For Us': Messianism and Redemption In The Work Of Walter Benjamin', in Cristaudo, Wayne & Baker, Wendy, editors, *Messianism Apocalypse & Redemption In 20th Century German Thought* (Adelaide: ATF Press, 2006).

Susin, Luiz Carlos, 'A Critique Of The Identity Paradigm', in *Concilium*, 55/2, Summer 2002.

Turner, Ian, editor, *The Australian Dream* (Melbourne: Sun Books, 1968).

White Patrick, *The Solid Mandala* (London: Eyre & Spottiswoode, 1966).

White Patrick, *The Vivisector* (London: Cape, 1970).

2

'Keep Your Mind In Hell And Despair Not.' *For The Term Of His Natural Life* And The Possibilities Of Isolation

It may seem odd to reflect on a novel about isolation of the most extreme kind, the hell of the convict system in Van Diemen's Land, and to gain from it an insight into a deeper notion of community. But that, I suggest, is the possibility hinted at in the words of a Russian thinker Staretz Siloman which I have taken for my epigraph. As he sees it, existence is robbed of its weight and gravity when it is deprived of its *agon*.

Walter Benjamin made a similar point when, reflecting on the meaning of history in general, turned to what he called 'the tradition of the oppressed' in particular. He wrote that although the vanquished may have lost in war, they did not lose their history. For them it is true, 'those events are truly finished and lost to their *praxis* . . . Victory bears its fruits entirely differently from the way in which defeat has its consequences' (Mertens, 2006: 76). Nevertheless, he argues, past suffering lays another claim on the present and this is the claim I would like to explore in Marcus Clarke's novel about this system. *For The Term Of His Natural Life* was itself a work of historical remembrance since it was written after the system of transportation had ended.

Remembrance, as Benjamin also points out, can modify what the events themselves seemed to have determined. Hannah Arendt writes in similar vein when she remarks that human society began with crime. 'Whatever brotherhood human beings may be capable of has grown out of fratricide, whatever political organization men may have achieved has its origins in crime' (Arendt, 1973: 20), in injustice particularly. Certainly non-Aboriginal Australia had such a beginning. But from it, I suggest, there developed a search for a different kind of community, the kind, I suggest, articulated, however awkwardly, at the end of the nineteenth century in the ideal of a 'fair go' for all and the notion of 'mateship'. In recent times it has fallen into abeyance, perhaps because of a relentless focus on the future at the expense of a more troubling past which, to anticipate a central point to be made later, has lead to the neglect of an essential, if often unprofessed factor in the formation of authentic community. Benjamin calls this the 'theological', the 'refusal to accept the finality of past suffering' and the determination to redeem it (Mertens, 2006: 75).

For The Term Of His Natural Life, as we have said, is a work of this kind of remembrance. It is the more powerful, I think, because it is a work of fiction and thus able to explore possibilities beyond rational comprehension, and the otherwise unspeakable, since they belong to the realm of the unconscious, 'the archaic, the nocturnal and the oneiric' (Ricoeur, 1969: 348). These things often shape events and people more deeply than we realise. That is why in my discussion of Clarke's novel I want first of all to refer to a passage in another work about imprisonment, Primo Levi's *If This Is A Man* (Levi, 1987) for it illuminates the theme of community which runs through *For The Term Of His Natural Life*. The book is an account of his experiences as a prisoner in a Nazi concentration camp.

Both works, as we have said, are about imprisonment and both insist on the isolation of a situation in which each man exists alone. It is a world in which human community has all but disappeared, a world ruled by force without the moderating influence of law. In this sense it is worse than Dante's hell, which is central to the passage from Levi's book on which I wish to focus. Dante's hell was at least governed by a certain proportion between the crime committed and its punishment. This was not so in the Nazi camps or in Clarke's novel: Dawes, the central character of Clarke's novel, is in fact an innocent man who is being punished for another's crime. In both places, therefore, authority was brutal or stupid or complacent, 'virtue a mere name' (Clarke, 2002: 240) and existence (in Levi's words), 'a bible of pain' (Levi, 1987: 83) subjecting them to degrading labour and brutal punishment for the slightest infractions. There was no comfort even from the natural world. Levi's account is full of the torments of winter's cold and Clarke describes Van Diemen's Land as a savage and unfamiliar place on the other side of the world whose coast, lashed by howling winds and cold, looked like 'a biscuit at which rats have been nibbling' (Clarke, 2002: 97). How then did the shape of a different kind of community emerge from these appalling beginnings?

This is where what I take to be the central passage in Levi's work is illuminating. It comes towards the end of his time in the camp. It is mid winter and he and a fellow prisoner, like him 'engaged in a personal and secret battle against the camp and death' (Levi, 1987: 143), are carrying the bucket of soup which is their ration from the kitchen to the hut they occupy with their fellow prisoners. Suddenly a scene from Dante's *Divine Comedy* comes to his mind, the scene in the depths of hell, in Canto XXVI of the *Inferno* in which the poet and Virgil, his guide, meet the Greek hero Ulysses. It is a poignant moment as Ulysses recalls the moment when after several attempts when he and his crew finally sailed through the Pillars of Hercules out of the Mediterranean into the open sea beyond. The description of the mountain they see on the shore just before they are overwhelmed by a sudden whirlwind reminds Levi of the mountain near his home when he, too, was a free man.

According to most commentators this is a crucial moment in Dante's journey. Like Ulysses, he has longed to 'experience . . . that which lies beyond/the sun, and . . . the world that is unpeopled'. But he is in hell precisely for this reason: he has overreached himself and is being punished for sacrilege, for defying the fact that human beings are not autonomous but belong to a cosmic order whose laws they must obey. This is not the way we imagine things today. For us the individual is free, sometimes almost obliged, to realise his/her desires wherever they may lead. But recalling this passage in the mindless, soulless vacuum of the camp, Levi is suddenly nostalgic for Dante's vision which now seems 'so human, so necessary and so neglected'. It presupposes a 'gigantic reality' beyond the self 'which perhaps contains the explanation of our destiny and our presence here' (Levi, 1987: 151). For this reason it should 'concern everyone who suffers' (Levi, 1987: 149), since we are all responsible for and to one another. Defying this reality the Nazis have created the hell in which he finds himself.

The sense that this community of mutual responsibility and respect is essential for a proper humanity is also, I suggest, the central point that Clarke's novel makes, even if here only three people, Dawes, Sylvia, the daughter of the commandant of the settlement, and North, one of the two chaplains, achieve it. Dawes is the first to catch a glimpse of it, though it is Sylvia, at this stage a mere child, who shows it to him. Significantly, however, it is not revealed in words but in an event which challenges the system that imprisons him by suggesting that a different order is possible, one based not on brute force but on compassion and respect.

Dawes has just managed to escape from solitary confinement on an island off the larger penal settlement of Sarah Island when he stumbles on survivors of the ship wrecked while taking Sylvia away from the settlement under the escort of the officer Maurice Frere. On the run and half starved, he is a frightening figure and Frere responds aggressively.

But the child Sylvia, moved by compassion for him, offers him some of their dwindling supply of food. This is a turning point for Dawes. The inscription over the gates of Dante's Hell read 'Abandon hope, all you who enter here'. But Sylvia's gesture tells him that goodness still exists and kindles the hope that he may yet belong again to the community of human beings. According to Theodor Adorno, this kind of hope is 'the only philosophy which can be responsibly practised in the face of despair' since it involves an 'attempt to contemplate all things as they would present themselves from the standpoint of redemption' and thus resists current reality by negating it (Kaufmann, 2006: 36).

The word 'redemption' here, of course, has theological overtones and may therefore seem unfashionable. But, if we define theology, as Martin Marty does, as a 'mode of awareness that evokes a transcendence of other transcendences . . . [by prompting] a way of attending to human experience from a perspective beyond our life world' (Hill, 2003: 187), then the impact Sylvia's gesture makes on Dawes is theological. It also liberates him from his isolation, from 'the dismal hermitage of his mind' (Clarke, 2002: 128). He regains the 'air of independence and authority' (Clarke, 2002: 178) which had been his when he was a free man and becomes an active and effective member of this small community of castaways. In fact, he proves himself a better man than Frere—in this situation rank counts for nothing—by guiding the party back to the settlement. But it is an achievement at his own expense.

Once there, the system takes over. Frere regains his authority, lies about Dawes' behaviour and claims all the credit for their rescue. Dawes is returned to captivity and punished for his escape.

Implicitly a contrast is drawn here between two different kinds of community, what Augustine calls the 'City of Man' which is based on love of self at the expense of the other—the community to which Frere subscribes—and the 'City of God' which Dawes has discovered, based on love of the other at the expense of the self. In passing, it is worth noting that this distinction may suggest that what we see as our present 'era of increased connectivity' may be moving in the opposite direction, to the extent that in it there are signs of increasing exploitation of and disconnection with the other. If this is so, then it is worth exploring the kind of community which Dawes glimpsed, as Levi did, even in the hell in which he found himself. This is especially the case, I would argue, if the tradition of a 'fair go', that is of this kind of community which developed in this country, may have derived from similar beginnings in reaction to the convict system.

Essentially, this community does not rely on institutions or on the power of the state but originates from below, in what Walter Benjamin calls 'the tradition of the oppressed' (Mertens, 2006: 74), from the hope for a better world. In *For The Term Of His Natural Life* the third member of this kind of community is an unexpected figure, the clergyman North, who is supposedly an establishment figure. In contrast from the other chaplain at the penal settlement, the obsequious Meekin, he is appalled by the injustices of the system and protests against them. Perhaps this is because he himself is acquainted with suffering, being a secret alcoholic. But distanced in this way from 'decent society' enables him to 'see around the corner where a different, unfamiliar life [is] . . . going on' (Day, 2006: 41), helping him to take his beliefs as a

Christian seriously rather than merely socially, as Meekin does. Here Clarke may be evoking Nietzsche's proposition that Christianity is the religion of slaves.

North's protests against the system reach a climax when a young convict, Kirkland, is flogged to death and he goes to the commandant to demand an inquiry. The commandant, Sylvia's father, is basically decent. But he is a servant of the system. So, like the Germans Hannah Arendt describes who went along with Hitler, resisting the 'temptation of doing good' (Arendt, 1994: 150), he refuses, on the grounds that an inquiry would take too long and cost too much. In reply, North appeals to the 'concept of something that would differ from the unspeakable world that is' (Kaufmann, 2006: 41), the belief that every human being is absolutely valuable and that we are all responsible for one another. North tells the commandant that '[n]o trouble, no expense, no dissatisfaction, should stand in the way of humanity and justice' (Clarke, 2002: 331).

His vehemence, however, is partly fuelled by self-disgust since at the time of the flogging he was too drunk to attend, as he should have done. This disgust is increased by the behaviour of Dawes, ordered to flog the boy, who refuses half way to continue and is himself savagely punished as a consequence. So when he hears this, North goes to see Dawes in his solitary confinement, confesses his failure and asks the convict to forgive him. At this moment, Dawes glimpses 'a misery more profound than his own' (328) but also once more realises, as he did in Sylvia's gesture years before, that goodness still exists. A bond grows up between them. When North visits him again, Dawes tells him how he came to be here, and that he has been convicted for a murder he did not commit. Listening to his story, North realises that he, the chaplain, is responsible since he had arrived on the murder scene first. But instead of pursuing the murderer, he had made off with the dead man's wallet, needing money to pay off his gambling debts and leaving Dawes, who arrived shortly afterwards, to be arrested for the murder. To add to his pain, Dawes realises that North is in love with Sylvia who, now a grown woman, is unhappily married to Frere.

In realistic terms, these coincidences are not easy to accept. But as far as our argument is concerned, they create a community of mutual respect between the two men and for North a sense of responsibility for the sufferings of the other. He decides, therefore, to make reparation, to let Dawes take his place on the ship which is also about to take Sylvia away. To refer to Benjamin once again, he would argue that North's situation here can only be properly resolved in what he calls 'theological' terms which make it possible for guilt to lead to 'grace, redemption and sacrifice' (Mertens, 2006: 63). By leaving the door of Dawes' cell open when he leaves, and leaving his own cloak behind for Dawes to use so that the boatman will mistake Dawes for himself, North sacrifices his own freedom and position.

As it happens, the ship sinks in a cyclone and Dawes and Sylvia are drowned. But this, it could be said, points to the insight that the kind of community envisaged here demands a radical break with the world it describes, pointing to possibilities as yet unrealised. The description of the last moments of Sylvia and Dawes, I think, suggests a 'transvaluation of value' of this kind: 'In the great crisis of our life, when, brought face to face with annihilation, we are suspended gasping over the great emptiness of death, we become conscious that the Self we thought we knew so well has strange and unthought of capacities' (Clarke, 2002: 537).

The language and tenor here may not be fashionable. But it makes a point worth reflection, Benjamin's point, that the consequences of defeat are different from the fruits of victory and that the 'losers' may have a meaning yet to be realised and that this meaning may need to be reworked by remembrance. At the very least, it returns us to Adorno's argument, that the only knowledge that can be responsibly practised in the face of despair is one which offers hope of redemption. If we are to continue to contest it, one must interrogate 'the world as it is, revealing it to be . . . as indigent and as distorted at it will appear one day' (Kaufmann, 2006: 36).

It also underlines the fact that the kind of alternative community represented by Dawes, Sylvia and North may be central to that hope.

This may seem utopian. But Benjamin's reflections on history, especially his discussion of the ideology of 'progress'—central, of course, to the culture of consumption, growth and technological efficiency—suggest that it is not. He sees progress as a storm which is relentlessly driving us into a future over which we have no control 'while the mountain of devastation before [our] eyes grows to high heaven'. But the angel of history's face is turned towards the past. Where *we* see a chain of events, *he* sees one single catastrophe, which incessantly heaps ruin upon ruin and slings them in front of his feet. He would like to resist the storm so as to stay, to wake the dead and to restore what has been torn asunder (Mertens, 2006: 73).

But that restoration, Benjamin suggests, depends upon the rediscovery of the 'theological'. This is a dimension to do not with having, which rules our present culture, but with being which he represents as the dwarf in the chess machine of history. It is a reality 'which is small and ugly nowadays, and cannot show itself under any circumstances'. Nevertheless, in his view, it 'animates and manipulates the outward machinery which represents historical materialism' (Mertens, 2006: 76), since it points beyond it to the 'quest for happiness of a free humanity' (Mertens, 2006: 69).

To conclude. I have been arguing that *For The Term Of His Natural Life* makes a similar point to Benjamin, as also to Primo Levi's *If this Is A Man*. It challenges the convict system's culture of disconnection, implying instead that in the long run a human community properly rests on concern for, rather than exploitation of, the other. As Emmanuel Levinas argues, a society which 'wipes out all otherness by murder or by all-encompassing and totalising thought . . . or war and politics' is ultimately unsustainable. It is 'only in the laying down by the ego of its sovereignty (in its 'hateful' modality), that we find ethics and . . . the meaning of being, that is, its appeal for justification' (Hand, 1993: 85). To reflect on the past, on the convict system in Van Diemen's Land or on the Nazi prison camps, on those apparently defeated by history, may therefore be important for any discussion of the good society.

References

Arendt, Hannah, *Eichmann In Jerusalem: A Report On The Banality Of Evil* (Camberwell: Penguin, 1994).

Arendt, Hannah, *On Revolution* (Ringwood: Penguin, 1973).

Clarke, Marcus, *For The Term Of His Natural Life* (Sydney: AR Classics, 2002).

Day, Frances, 'The Fate Of Hope In Hollow Spaces: Ernst Bloch's Messianism', in Cristaudo, Wayne & Baker, Wendy editors, *Messianism Apoca-lypse & Redemption In 20th Century German Thought* (Adelaide: ATF Press, 2006).

Hand, Sean, editor, *The Levinas Reader* (Oxford: Blackwell, 1993).

Hill, Jack, 'Images Of Religion In South Pacific Fiction: An Interpretation Of *Pouliuli*', in *Literature And Theology*, 17/2, June 2003.

Kaufmann, David, 'In The Light Of "The Light of Transcendence": Redemption In Adorno', in Cristaudo, Wayne, & Baker, Wendy editors, *Messianism Apocalypse & Redemption In 20th Century German Thought* (Adelaide: ATF Press, 2006).

Levi, Primo, *Se Questo E Un Uomo, Si C'est Un Homme* (Paris: Julliard, 1987). The translation into English is mine.

Mertens, Bram, '"Hope, Yes, But Not For Us": Messianism And Redemption In The Work Of Walter Benjamin', in Cristaudo, Wayne, & Baker, Wendy, editors, *Messianism Apocalypse & Redemption In 20th Century German Thought* (Adelaide: ATF Press, 2006).

Ricoeur, Paul, *The Symbolism Of Evil* (Boston: Beacon Press, 1969).

3

Human Distress And Suffering: The Question Of The Holocaust. Primo Levi's *If This Is A Man*

Literature has an abiding concern with human suffering, not because suffering is a good thing but because it is not, and should not be. Suffering is an offence against our notions of justice. It may be true that, destruction as well as creation is the law of life as a whole. But what we hope is that in the long run creation will prevail. This is a truth which literature attempts to explore. There is no time here to survey the range of works of this kind. Instead let us focus on one work, Primo Levi's account of his sufferings as a prisoner in Auschwitz, *Se Questo E Un Uomo* (*If This Is A Man*), a work which he wrote, he said, to liberate himself at last from his memories by staring them down and confronting the questions they pose (Levi, 1987). In the long run, perhaps, he did not succeed since, years later, still haunted, he committed suicide. Nevertheless, the record he left of his struggle to survive remains profoundly illuminating.

The work is also the stuff of tragedy, even if it is not written in tragic form. Certainly, the title, *If This Is A Man*, poses the essential tragic question: how can human dignity be sustained in the face of overwhelming suffering? In fact the book is a record of courage, the determination not to give way before such suffering. But it also suggests the way in which courage renders suffering less intolerable, and endows it with tragic dignity, as the individual appeals away from the disastrous present to a perspective beyond history in which a more expansive notion of justice may be found. In a time like ours, this kind of appeal to an order beyond the self, and its desires and understanding, the kind of understanding which is the stuff of classical tragedy and of works like the *The Book Of Job*, seems increasingly difficult to sustain. But that, I suggest, is the reason why Levi's contribution is so important.

The situation he describes—in which he and thousands of others found themselves in Nazi concentration camps—is what Nietzsche described in his vision of a world in which God has ceased to exist. And making allowances for differences of scale, it also resembles the world today in which many people find themselves: solitary and straying 'as through an infinite space . . . feeling the breath of [this] empty space' in which direction and meaning no longer have disappeared (Kaufmann, 1968: 95). All that existed, it seemed, subjected as they were to the brutalities of a system intent on their humiliation and destruction, were pain, hunger, cold and exhaustion.

Without purpose or meaning each suffered alone without hope of release, trapped in a machine designed to exterminate them, forgotten by the rest of the world. Friends and country left behind, they existed beyond the pale of reason and decency in which 'there [was] no where or even why' (Levi, 1987: 4), ruled by a 'geometric madness' (Levi, 1987: 64) which was determined to rob its victims of dignity and hope and reduce them to a 'stupor' (Levi, 1987: 16). No alternative seemed possible since it was a world without passion. As Levi recalled it, for example, even when the guards struck them they did so mechanically, showing no emotion. It was as if they were the victims of a 'wickedness beyond evil', of an ethical collapse which rendered their tormentors unable to comprehend what they were doing or take any responsibility for it.

The suffering of their victims was metaphysical as well as physical to the extent that this evil was their environment. This kind of suffering is what Simone Weil called 'affliction', a sense of urootedness, as if one is already dead to what is properly human and is filled with self-disgust at this condition (Weil, 1959: 118). The question implicit in the title of Levi's book, *If This Is A Man*, suggests this kind of suffering. The fate of the people he describes—those robbed of dignity, hope and any real power to resist it—lacks the splendour of tragedy since choice has nothing to do with their situation. A figure like Lear, for example, is in a sense responsible for his fate so that there is a certain justice involved since he had overstepped the limit, claiming limitless power for himself and demanding absolute obedience to his desires. Levi and others, however, were overwhelmed by forces completely beyond their control and overwhelmed by the brutality, the 'venomous fruit' (Levi, 1987: 262), of a system based on hatred and mindless fear, the *ressentiment* which Nietzsche saw as the revolt of slaves but which Levi believed is a 'latent infection in all of us'.

What makes affliction of this kind so devastating is that goodness and justice no longer seem to exist. It is the world Nietzsche's madman described in which God is dead. We have murdered him and are now 'straying as through an infinite nothing' (Kaufmann, 1968: 95). What is important about Levi's book, however, is that even here he manages to recover his dignity and even find hope in the midst of his suffering, glimpsing a kind of meaning in it. In our present context, I think, this matters because many, if not most people in affluent societies like ours, are afflicted by the apparent meaningless of their suffering or of the suffering of others.

Levi's revelation comes, significantly, from literature, from a discovery of a resource within our culture which enables him to draw new meaning from old definitions which no longer seem appropriate, a meaning directed to a goodness that transcends our current ability to understand what it is. The passage is from Dante's *Inferno* in which Dante meets Ulysses in the depths of hell who then tells him how he came to be there. In the freezing middle of winter, as Levi and another prisoner on canteen duty were carrying the daily ration of soup through the snow from the kitchen to the hut in which their fellows were waiting, this passage suddenly and inexplicably came into his mind. Ulysses begins with the exultant moment as he and his crew sailed through the Pillars of Hercules into the ocean and a new and unknown world opened out before them. This is for Levi a painful moment as he is moved by the distance between this instance of liberation, and of new possibilities opening out before Ulysses and his crew, and the situation which he and his fellow prisoners must endure. Ulysses' mention of the mountain they glimpsed inland as they sailed through the straits, increases this pain since it reminds Levi of mountain he used to see in the distance when he was returning home as a free man.

Ulysses' address to his crew at this moment seems at first to intensify the contrast:

> Brothers,' I said, 'O you, who having crossed
> a hundred thousand dangers, reach the west,
> to this brief waking time that still is left
> unto your senses, you must not deny
> experience of that which lies beyond
> the sun, and of the world that is unpeopled.
> Consider well the seed that gave you birth;
> You were not made to live your lives as brutes,
> But to be followers of worth and knowledge (Dante, 1982: 245).

But then, as Levi reflected on these words, he seemed to be hearing them for the first time. It was as if they rang out 'like trumpets, like the voice of God' (Levi, 1987: 149) reminding him, in the midst of his exhaustion and despair, of the resolve he had made when he first arrived at Auschwitz, never to submit to or inwardly accept the monstrous regime which had imprisoned him (Levi, 1987: 65). The words, 'you were not made to live your lives like brutes', reminded him of the belief he once had in his essential dignity as a human being. But Ulysses' exhortation to his men which follows was even more rousing, calling them to explore 'the world that is unpeopled', one which 'lies beyond the sun', pointing to some vast imperishable world elsewhere which we are born to explore. This, he suddenly realised, applied not only to him but also to all who suffer.

Disastrous as it first appears, what happened next to Ulysses and his men extended this realisation:

> ... [O]ut of that new land a whirlwind rose
> and hammered at our ship, against her bow.
> Three times it turned her round with all the waters;
> and at the fourth, it lifted up the stern,
> so that our prow plunged deep, as pleased an Other,
> until the sea again closed—over us (Dante, 1982: 244).

The phrase 'as pleased an Other' is the key. It suggests that there is a logic to Ulysses' fate since a larger order exists which 'lies beyond the sun' in which it makes sense. This is the kind of insight Job also reaches at the end of his story when he bows down before 'things too wonderful for me, which I did not know' (Job 42:3). At this moment, Levi, who had been reciting the passage to his companion, broke off, telling him that it was absolutely critical that he listen intently to the passage, that he must understand the significance of the phrase, 'as pleased an Other', before it was too late. It might seem anachronistic, but these words from the long past Middle Ages nevertheless contained the explanation of their destiny and their presence here (Levi, 1987: 151).

As Levi realised, few of us today in a desacralised culture believe in this 'Other' whose power and logic we must accept. For most of us, the individual is seen as self-sufficient and more or less obliged to realise his/her desires wherever they may lead. But in this passage, Dante implies that we human beings are part of cosmic order and owe obedience to its laws. So, for him, Ulysses' fate is understandable. He is being punished for sacrilege, for defying this order and asserting his desires against it and therefore bears some responsibility for his fate, giving it some meaning and dignity. According to Levi, this incident enabled him to survive. Not that he could share Dante's belief. But he was able to glimpse the possibility of some order, a justice and goodness beyond history and beyond his understanding. Faith in this order rather than in history demands courage. But it may be the best that is possible in the midst of suffering since it makes it possible to avoid despair. This is not easy, of course. As Emmanuel Levinas puts it, 'modern man persists in his being as a sovereign who is . . . concerned to maintain the powers of his sovereignty' (Hand, 1993: 78), believing that the world should serve his/her needs and demands. But the fate of Levi and thousands, possibly millions, like him in the world today, experiencing physical and mental suffering and death, suggest that this is a destructive and dangerous illusion. To sustain ourselves we must attempt to live a life we do not understand and find some hope in looking beyond our present understanding.

In effect, this is a view which could be called theological, since it involves the recognition of some mysterious authority beyond the self, the authority of existence itself. As we have said, this is not a fashionable position today; many indeed would see it as dishonest and even disreputable. It is significant, however, that in the 1930s, in the midst of the Great Depression and the growing power of Nazism, Fascism and Stalinism, thinkers like Walter Benjamin and later, in the aftermath of the Second World War, Hannah Arendt and Karl Jaspers, seemed also to be making a similar response. Disillusioned with the direction in which contemporary history was moving—Arendt's partner, Heinrich Blucher, for instance, saw it as a 'societal maelstrom' which was creating 'a boiling mass of ghost like, solitary individuals' (Arendt, 1992: 278)—they were echoing Nietzsche's denunciation of 'the "true world"'. They believed that such a world must be abolished and called for a 'transvaluation of value'. Blucher was particularly scornful of the notion of 'progress'. This preoccupation with the future was not only prepared to sacrifice the present to its demands but it also ignored the wisdom of the past, as if, he wrote, 'a future could ever open up for human beings who have lost sight of eternity' (Arendt, 1992: 278). Levi also came to suspect the same as he recalled Dante's insight.

But it is perhaps Walter Benjamin's work that is most relevant here. Like Levi, he was Jewish. The last phase of his work could be seen as a response to Nazism—in fact he died on the border between France and Spain attempting to escape from Nazism. He too was appalled by what he saw as the 'storm of history' driving towards the future, leaving behind a pile of ruins (Mertens, 2006: 73). The only hope he saw in it was theology, a belief in the trans-historical reality that Levi also glimpsed. Comparing it to a dwarf, 'small and ugly nowadays which cannot show itself under any circumstance', he nevertheless believed that ultimately it animates and manipulates the course of human affairs (Mertens, 2006: 69). The reason for this belief brings us back to Levi since he saw the human lot as a 'communion of suffering'—a view very different from the idea of history as 'progress', usually defined in material terms.

For Benjamin, therefore, it was not the 'winners' but the losers who mattered. Their fate had a meaning as yet unrealised which, once understood, would take the human story in a different direction. This meaning, he thought, would be only intelligible to theological categories since these categories alone, as his friend and colleague Theodor Adorno wrote, offered the hope of 'something that would differ from the unspeakable world that is' (Kaufmann, 2006: 41). This, I would argue, is the kind of hope Levi glimpsed in the midst of apparent hopelessness of his situation, the hope of some larger order.

It also suggests that, like Benjamin, he recognised a 'community of suffering'. This was a crucial matter in his sense of isolation from the rest of humanity—having to suffer alone was one of the worst of his sufferings. But he describes with something like awe, for instance, an incident one freezing night when one of his fellow prisoners got out of his bunk to care for another who was dying of dysentery and lying on the floor in his own mess. He cleaned him, using his own ragged shirt to do so. The prostrate man may have seemed physically disgusting but this gesture recognised his dignity as a human being, the kind of recognition which is the due of all those who suffer in any way. Other acts of kindness and concern, infrequent as they were, pointed beyond the 'unspeakable world' in which they were imprisoned —and sustained him.

According to Adorno, such gestures expressed 'the only philosophy that can be responsibly practised in the face of despair . . . the attempt to contemplate all things as they would present themselves from the standpoint of redeem-ption' (Kaufmann, 2006: 36). It is important to note that, 'redemption' is being seen here as a recognition of an abiding order elsewhere, the 'eternity' that Blucher invoked against the history of 'progress' in whose perspective even a man dying in squalor demands respect and care. As Simone Weil would see it, this was a moment of the 'grace' which she sets over against the 'gravity' of brutal physical necessity, an illumination which penetrates to the centre of the self, permeating its whole being. It conquers the brutal meaninglessness of suffering with the intuition that ultimately goodness and justice, incomprehensible as it may seem, still exists (Weil, 1959: 118–19). It is this kind of grace, I suggest, which comes to Lear in his last moments when Cordelia bends over him and he sees the love and forgiveness in her eyes, bringing with it a joy so powerful that it breaks his heart. It may be too much for him, but Adorno writes that the hope this grace brings, 'wrested from reality by negating it', is nevertheless the only form in which truth may appear in the midst of such extreme suffering (Kaufamnn, 2006: 35).

For Lear, and other tragic figures like Othello and Oedipus, it is true that grace comes too late and the distance between this truth, and their situation, proves unendurable. But for Levi, to return to him, the possibility of an order other than the brutal one intent on destroying him and the people to whom he belongs, enables him to endure. In its light, it seems as if his tormenters are not merely criminals but also fools who are not properly human (Levi, 1987: 128). So it matters profoundly that he should bear his sufferings and if possible survive.

But what of people suffering in less extreme situations, especially if their suffering is not, as his were, clearly the result of human malevolence? How is it possible for someone grieving the loss of a child or suffering from cancer, for instance, to believe in an ultimate order which is good and just?

Simone Weil has useful things to say about this problem. According to her 'the great enigma of human life is not suffering but affliction', a feeling of meaninglessness which 'stamps the soul to its very depths with the scorn, the disgust and even the self-hatred and sense of guilt and defilement that crime logically should produce'. Affliction breeds a feeling of being an outcast socially and psychologically, uprooted from life in 'a more or less attenuated equivalent of death' (Weil, 1959: 129). But she goes on to point to the kind of hope that we have been discussing: the hope that this misery may point to a presence beyond the perception of reason or commonsense, to a meaning and a greater plenitude than the presence of all worldly entities, to the 'things too wonderful for me, which I did not know' (Weil, 1959: 131), which Job finally acknowledged and which justified his refusal to surrender his dignity. 'All the horrors produced in the world', Weil argues, 'are like the folds imposed on the waves by gravity' (Weil, 1959: 131). But beyond this physical necessity there is the necessity imposed by these 'things too wonderful' for us.

This may seem an unpalatable way of dealing with the problem of suffering. But it may be realistic. For Weil, just as 'one has to learn to read or to practice a trade, so one must learn to feel in all things . . . the obedience of the universe to God' (Weil, 1959: 131), that is to some ultimate reality beyond our understanding. It seems to me that this is the insight offered by tragedy as well as by faith. To return to *If This Is A Man*, it is clear that Levi recovered hope when he caught a glimpse of this ultimately 'unreasonable reason'. It was this which sustained and empowered him in his 'personal and secret battle against the camp and death' (Levi, 1987: 143), enabling him to live, as Regina Schwartz understands Levinas, with a 'full conscience [under an] empty sky' (Schwartz, 2002: 381–2).

References

Dante, *The Divine Comedy Of Dante Alighieri*, translated by Allen Mandelbaum (New York: Bantam Books, 1982).

Hand, Sean, editor, *The Levinas Reader* (Oxford: Blackwell, 1993).

Kaufmann, David, 'In The Light Of "The light Of Transcendence": Redemption In Adorno', in Cristaudo, Wayne & Baker, Wendy, editors, *Messianism Apocalypse & Redemption In 20th Century German Thought* (Adelaide: ATF Press, 2006).

Kaufmann, Walter, editor, *The Portable Nietzsche* (Ringwood: Penguin, 1968).

Kohler, Lotte, and Hans Saner, Hans, editors, *Correspondence Hannah Arendt Karl Jaspers* (New York: Harcourt Brace Harvest Book, 1992).

Levi, Primo, *Si C'est Un Homme* (Paris: Julliard, 1987).

Mertens, Bram, '"Hope, Yes, But Not For Us": Messianism And Redmption in the work of Walter Benjamin', in Cristaudo, Wayne & Baker, Wendy, editors, *Messianism Apocalypse & Redemption In 20th Century German Thought* (Adelaide: ATF Press, 2006).

Schwartz, Regina, 'Revelation And Revolution', in *Cross Currents*, 56/3 2006.

Weil, Simone, *Waiting For God* (New York: Capricorn Books, 1959).

4

The Dragon Slayer: Patrick White And History

Let me use two quotations to frame my argument. The first is Vita Sackville West's answer when asked whether she wrote about the 'real world': 'Certainly not! One of the damn things is enough'. The second is from Nietzsche's *Twilight Of The Idols:* 'the "true" world—an idea which is no longer good for anything, not even obligating—an idea which has become useless and superfluous—*consequently*, a refuted idea: let us abolish it!' (Kaufmann, 1981: 485). I want to argue that Patrick White's work should be set in this context. Call it modernist or post-modernist as you like, but what is central to it is its rejection of what most of us would regard as the 'real world', in favour of one which enables the 'state of silence, simplicity and humility', which White regarded as the only proper one for human beings (White, 1958: I, 1).

His early critics were disapprovingly aware of this. Again two examples will have to do. Reviewing *Voss* Kylie Tennant, for instance, wrote: 'When the book strikes off into the deserts of mysticism, I am one of those people who would sooner slink off home' (Tennant, 1958: 12). A decade later Peter Wood found an absence in White's novels of 'issues we can take seriously at an adult level' (Wood, 1962: 22), issues, that is, of a metaphysical kind. In effect, their home was the 'real world'. White was aware of this, but, unlike Nietzsche, he no longer found it useless and no longer obligating. He attacked the 'dun coloured realism' of most Australian novels and people who believed only in what they could see, touch and calculate. These were the Mr Bonners of this world, those who clung to the fringes of the self as they clung to the fringes of the continent, wanting to be 'safe in life, safe in death' (White, 1971: 349).

I suggest that it is useful to situate White in the context of thinkers, such as Adorno and Benjamin and later Arendt and Jaspers. These writers all wanted to interrupt what they saw as the disastrous course of history and the state of emergency it had created and wrench it on to a new course, one that would create a new sense of self and of reality. According to Michael Taussig, they saw a world, under 'the spell of death and terror', one in which understanding 'was frozen and naturalized in . . . a *still life* or landscape' and therefore catastrophically enthralled by things (Taussig, 2006: 27). Significantly, as White tells us in *Flaws In The Glass*, he had spent time in Germany in the 1930s and served in the Second World War. *Voss*, for instance, was conceived during the African desert campaign reflecting on Hitler's madness, in effect echoing Jasper's interrogation of the 'false grandeur' which contemporary history had 'stolen from God' (Kohler, 1993: 148).

White's second novel, *The Living And The Dead*, published in 1941, is preoccupied with contemporary history and with revulsion against what Sartre called the sheer is-ness of what is seen as the 'real world'. It opens at a London railway station as Elyot Standish is saying goodbye to his sister on her way to join the war in Spain (where her lover has been killed). He noticed a young Jewish woman nearby whose husband is leaving for Europe, and is drawn 'into a region where the present dissolved, its forms and purpose, became a shapeless, directionless well of fear'. Later, on his way home, he watches helplessly as a drunk falls under a bus, an image, if you like of Benjamin's world 'under the spell of death and terror . . . frozen and naturalised'. This is a world which, Elyot feels, has 'no respect for personal existence', and one in which he 'hadn't the power to restore a pretence of life' (White, 1967: 7).

This sense of fatedness, waste and disgust, pervades the novel. But Elyot's sister, significantly named Eden, rebels against it and, in my view, foreshadows the direction White's work is to take when she declares to her lover as he is about to leave for Spain:

> I believe . . . but not in the parties of politics . . . a change from wrong to right, which has nothing to do with category . . . I want to unite those who have the capacity for living, in any circumstance, and make it the one circumstance. I want to oppose them to the dealers in words, to the diseased, to the most fatally diseased—the indifferent. That can be the only order. Without ideological limits. Labels set a limit at once. And there is no limit to man (253–4).

This echoes Lawrence at his clumsiest, so it is not surprising that, later, White found this novel embarrassing. But, awkward as it may seem, it expresses his sense of post-war Europe as an 'aching wilderness, in which the ghosts of Homer, St Paul and Tolstoy sat waiting for the crash' (White, 1958: 146). Nevertheless, it also reflects Karl Jasper's belief that 'the one great opportunity' to change the course of this disastrous history, lay in an appeal to 'human existence itself' by 'remaining loyal to reality though good and ill' (Kohler, 1993: 2087). How reality is defined is the crucial question, of course.

Clearly, White was disgusted by the language of a culture which 'rests on the exaltation of signs based on the denial of the reality of things'—and of people (Baudrillard, 1990: 63), the language of metonymy, the self-referential language which reinforces this culture. Instead, he invented a language which was exploratory, the kind of language Adorno compared to 'a child at the piano searching for a chord never previously heard . . . [a] chord, however, [which] was always there [since] the possible combinations are limited [so that] . . . everything that can be played on it are implicitly given in the keyboard' (Hughes, 2004: 478). This is the language of metaphor and symbol, which points away from surface appearances, providing access to what is otherwise inexpressible, the 'archaic, the nocturnal, the oneiric' (Ricoeur, 1969: 348). Thus it opens out the possibility of different kinds of reality and value, a glimpse if you like of the 'grandeur too overwhelming to express' which he was seeking to express in his work.

This possibility appears even in the otherwise miserable world of *The Living And The Dead* in one of its few positive moments when Elyot as a boy is on holidays at Ard's Bay:

> It was an almost enclosed, almost circular bay. He spent many hours looking into pools. There were crabs. There were red, blunt anemones and the paler, trailing kind. He took up the smooth stones in his hand, the red and mauve stones, that shone when you took them out of the water. And standing on the rim of the bay, holding the rounded stones in his hand, everything felt secure . . . You looked into water and saw the shape of things (101–2).

This is what the painter Hurtle Duffield in *The Vivisector* hoped to achieve in his work, a moment 'in which dreams and facts had been locked in an architecture which did not appear alterable' (White, 1970: 217). This moment is one which moves beyond surface appearances, revealing further, possibly infinite, possibilities as meaning and being are somehow united, even if the meaning involved cannot be put into words. It was thus a glimpse of plenitude, an alternative to what Heinrich Blucher called the 'maelstrom' of history 'driven by interests, that sucks us down into its depths', sweeping us 'from humanity to nationality to bestiality' (Kohler, 1993: 278–9). But it is also the goal White was seeking in returning to Australia from 'the gothic shell of Europe': a 'state of silence, simplicity and humility' (White, 1958: 3, 38).

Moments like this, crucially important in all of White's subsequent novels, are often dismissed (as Kylie Tennant did) as merely 'mystical'. But they represent a response to contemporary history. This is clearest in the symbol of the chariot, central to *Riders In The Chariot*. It echoes the biblical prophet Ezechiel's vision of the chariot of divine power quitting the temple, the nation's centre, which has been destroyed as punishment for their infidelities. It is a departure that calls on them to change their ways. But it is also a reminder of Blake's chariot of fire, the portent of a 'new Jerusalem' which is to be built in England's 'green and sunny land' through the transforming power of an imagination able to 'see a world in a grain of sand . . . and eternity in an hour'.

Far from representing a retreat from historical reality, I would argue that they attempt to wrench it on to a different course, away from a culture of conquest and domination to a sense of the larger community of life. It is just as Hurtle Duffield realised, he 'was not his own dynamo' (White, 1970: 147). Similarly at the end of *The Tree Of Man*, Stan Parker sees himself as part of 'the large triumphal scheme of life' in which God is to be found even in a gob of spittle and that therefore 'One, and no other figure is the answer to all sums' (White, 1963: 474–7).

Many critics have attacked this move, rejecting it as 'theological' and thus an outrage to commonsense. But a good deal of evidence at the moment suggests the need for some kind of 'transvaluation of value' if we are to contest the history which is creating what Blucher calls a 'boiling mass society of ghost like, isolated individuals'. People like Mrs Flack and Mrs Jolley or the Bonners, White pillories in his work, these devotees of 'progress' and 'development'. They are all swept along, as Blucher says, 'from the past to the future by leaping over the present'—as if 'a future could ever open up for human beings who have lost sight of eternity' (Kohler, 1993: 278)—some abiding sense of value and reality, a 'still point of the turning world'.

It is they, White would say who are the ones out of touch with reality and devotees of religion, the type that Marx defined, 'the self-consciousness and self-regard of man who has either not yet found or who has already lost himself' (Easton, 1967: 250). They are trapped within the narrow confines of a culture dedicated to fantasies of power, possessions and pleasure. In contrast, the world White opens out is expansive, open to infinite possibility even in the lives of ordinary people like Stan Parker or Mrs Godbold or, at the other end of the social scale, Elizabeth Hunter or, apparent monsters, like Hurtle Duffield.

But the world they inhabit does not exist elsewhere in some imaginary future but, as two of the epigraphs to *The Solid Mandala* insist, 'in this one' and 'not outside . . . [but] inside: wholly within' the self (White, 1966), to be achieved by the transformative power of imagination which refuses to be manipulated from the outside and draws new meanings from old definitions of reality and value, exploring them more deeply. In this way White contests the direction of contemporary history, seeing progress not as increasing possessions, but as the move to deeper understanding, by renewing the transformative powers of a language which does not turn away from the pain of things, the terrors and squalor of our times. It embraces difficulty. But for this reason, because it refuses easy answers and false consolations, it is secure against loss, acknowledging the darkness we face but pointing a way through it.

References

Baudrillard, Jean, *Revenge Of The Crystal* (Sydney: Pluto Press, 1990).

Easton, Lloyd and Guddat, Kurt, *Writings Of The Young Marx On Philosophy And Society* (New York: Doubleday Anchor Book, 1967).

Hughes, John, 'Unspeakable Utopia: Art And The Return Of The Theological In The Marxism Of Adorno And Horkheimer', in *Cross Currents*, 53/4, Winter 2004.

Kaufmann, Walter, editor, *The Portable Nietzsche* (Ringwood: Penguin, 1981).

Kohler, Lotte and Saner, Hans, editors, *Correspondence Hannah Arendt Karl Jaspers 1926–1969* (New York: Harcourt Brace Harvester Book, 1993).

Ricoeur, Paul, *The Symbolism Of Evil* (Boston: Beacon Press, 1969).

Taussig, Michael, *Walter Benjamin's Grave* (London: University of Chicago Press, 2006).

Tennant, Kylie, 'Poetic Symbolism In a Novel By Patrick White', in *Sydney Morning Herald*, 8 February 1958.

White, Patrick, *The Aunt's Story* (London: Eyre & Spottiswoode, 1958, first published in 1948).

White, Patrick, *The Living And The Dead* (Ringwood: Penguin, 1967).

White, Patrick 'The Prodigal Son', in *Australian Letters*, I/1, 1958.

White, Patrick, *The Tree Of Man* (Ringwood: Penguin, 1963).

White, Patrick *The Solid Mandala* (London: Eyre & Spottiswoode, 1966).

White, Patrick, *The Vivisector* (London: Cape, 1970).

White, Patrick *Voss* (Ringwood: Penguin, 1971).

Wood, Peter, 'Moral Complexity In Patrick White's Novels', in *Meanjin*, XXI, 1962.

5

Borders, Identity And Australia

Though it may refer to physical features—the fact that Australia is 'girt by sea', for example—a border is really an imaginative construct, part of the construction of the 'imagined community' which is called a 'nation'. It can have both negative and positive connotations: as a mark of separation or, if used as a verb, the action of approaching or verging on another culture or environment. As it has been defined in this country since its beginnings as a settler society, however, border has usually been defined negatively as an expression and focus of anxiety about invasion from outside but also of subversion from within: witness the fear of 'the Yellow Peril', the White Australia Policy, attempts to destroy Aboriginal cultures, the race riots in Sydney's Cronulla beach a few years back, the treatment of asylum seekers, and so on.

Most settler societies, I suppose, belong to what Walter Benjamin has called the 'tradition of catastrophe'. They originated at a crucial moment of cultural disruption, a loss of faith in some of its certainties—by those involved in emigrating at least—and the acceptance of a need for change. This displacement, however, made for the kind of anxiety described in Henry Kingsley's *The Recollections Of Geoffrey Hamlyn*. First comes 'the disturbance of household gods, and the rupture of life-old associations' with the realization that, as Hamlyn put it, he was going

> to a land where none know me or care for me, [leaving] forever all that I know and love . . . Few know the feeling . . . of isolation, almost of terror, at having gone so far out of the bounds of ordinary life; the feeling of self-distrust and cowardice at being alone and friendless in the world, like a child in the dark (Mellick, 1982: 134-5).

As Luiz Carlos Susin points out, identity of this kind is based on the story of Ulysses who left home and traveled through strange and dangerous places, but always with the intention of returning home—as Hamlyn does, having redeemed the family fortunes in Australia—or of transforming these places into the equivalent of home, building 'a new Britannia in another world', as one early settler put it (Turner, 1968: 12). But, as Susin says, this 'Odyssey of the West' was 'not an authentic adventure . . . [but] a closed circle around sameness' (Susin, 2000: 87) in which difference is seen as threatening and must be destroyed or assimilated. Similarly, good and evil are defined in relation to the desires of the imperial self seen 'as basis and referent of the whole of reality, spread out at its feet' (Susin, 2000: 80). If this is recognised as the pattern underlying our society, the present concern with estab-lishing and defending borders is not surprising.

What we are dealing with, however, largely exists at the unconscious level and is mostly a matter of implicit assumption rather than explicit statement. Fiction can be a useful way of exploring these assumptions, to the extent that it uses symbolic rather than literal description. Symbols, Paul Ricoeur argues, provide access to the unconscious, to what is otherwise unspoken and often unspeakable since it belongs to the dimension of 'the archaic, the nocturnal, the oneiric' (Ricoeur, 1969: 348) and can thus function 'as surveyor's staff and guide' for understanding (Ricoeur, 1969: 13).

So I want to examine two recent works, Andrew McGahan's *The White Earth* and Kate Grenville's *The Secret River*. One explores the current preoccupation with borders, both external and internal, and the other is looking to move across them.

To consider McGahan's novel first, the central character, John McIvor, sees the world as a dark and dangerous place where evil lurks, threatening his security and possessions. This sense permeates the novel. Its opening image, for instance, is catastrophic: a dark cloud 'rolled and boiled as it climbed into the clear blue day, casting a vast shadow upon the hills beyond' and is compared to the mushroom cloud of a nuclear explosion (McGahan, 2004: 1). In fact, its cause is the explosion of a harvester which kills a farmer, but metaphorically at least, it does mark the end of his previous world for the boy who witnesses it, McIvor's nephew, William. His father was that farmer. This melodramatic opening sets the tone for the rest of the novel.

Melodrama, the conflict between absolute good and absolute evil, tends to arise within the 'closed circle around sameness'. *The White Earth*'s tone is melodramatic in this sense, full of apocalyptic images and situations of this kind. So McIvor, the dark repressive figure who dominates the novel resembles Heathcliff in *Wuthering Heights*—though he lacks his erotic appeal—a self-made man who believes himself beholden to no one. He is the typical 'imperial self', not concerned, as those who belong to traditional societies are, to find his place in the world but determined to remake that world according to his own image. When the world seems to be going in a direction he dislikes—when the government moves to legislate for Aboriginal Land Rights, for instance—he founds a movement and then organises a rally to oppose it. The charter of the movement is about defending Australia's borders and the 'White Man's Supremacy', on the one hand rejecting 'the United Nations and any other body that seeks to limit Australian sovereignty' and on the other attacking 'preferential treatment of elite minorities' (which McIvor, Pauline Hanson in real life—a political figure in Australia in the 1990's—largely identifies with Aboriginal Australians). The charter proclaims his belief in 'One Flag, One People, One Nation' (McGahan, 2004: 133)—a slogan which echoes Hitler's 'One Land, One Law, One People' (McGahan, 2004: 133). Underlying this is the belief that the land is his by right of conquest, in effect that might equals right and that dissent and difference must be suppressed.

Seen from the outside, however, this view is the product not only of ethical poverty but also of historical ignorance. Mere assertion like McIvor's that 'the Aborigines were gone and wouldn't be coming back' (McGahan, 2004: 100) is no proof that this is so. Indeed, the narrative suggests that it is not, since he is haunted by their continuing presence as well as by talk of Land Rights. Even his declaration to members of his movement—'"This is my property now. This is all your properties, your farms, your houses, your yards . . . We must be prepared to defend what we own . . . Australia—every square inch of it—it is *our* sacred site"' (McGahan, 2004: 209)—bespeaks their presence. This assertion also sits uneasily with his claim that he is defending 'the inherent value of Australian culture and traditions' since that culture and traditions necessarily includes those of the First Peoples who have inhabited this land from time immemorial. But in McIvor's mind, history belongs only to the 'winners', people like himself, and has no place for 'losers'.

Yet these assertions, the novel suggests, are the product of personal anxiety, even at the social level where he seems to have succeeded. As the owner of Kuran, the station which originally belonged to a pioneering family, he is an usurper. His father had been the manager but brought up his son to believe that one day he would take over the station by marrying the daughter of that family, their only child. But when his approaches are contemptuously dismissed, he sets himself to succeed by his own efforts, working obsessively to make the money to do so and sacrificing everything, including his marriage, in the process.

To use a distinction made by Helene Cixous (Moi, 1991: 111–12) this obsession with property is essentially 'masculine'—in contrast with the culture she calls 'feminine, which is open, ready to give and receive from others, is less preoccupied with external than with inner reality, with 'the resonance of fore-language', what is unspoken and often unconscious and is thus prepared to move across borders rather than defend them. McIvor, however, is perpetually on the defensive, determined to rely only on himself. As Cixous observes, in the 'masculine' economy, 'the moment you receive something you are effectively "open" to the other, [but] if you are a man, you have only one wish, and that is hastily to return the gift, to break the circuit of an exchange that could have no end . . . to be nobody's child, to owe no one a thing' (Moi, 1991: 110). I do not need, I think, to spell out the parallels with the policies of the government led by John Howard until November 2007 and the beliefs of its supporters.

Significantly, however, as the novel draws to its end, McIvor's nephew, William, is beginning to move in the opposite, 'feminine' direction, increasingly open to the 'fore-language' of the land as he explores Kuran and senses in it 'something powerful in its own right—to hear a voice in it, meant specifically for human ears' (McGahan, 2004: 100). But this voice also introduces him to a history different from the one which sustains his uncle's heroic explorers and pioneers, shepherds and stockmen, bush rangers and Diggers and so on. It suggests another set of images of 'deranged things, wrong things' (McGahan, 2004: 327) to do with the Aboriginal story. It speaks especially loudly at the spring from which, significantly, the main river system of the country originates, but into which, in the past, the bodies of the Aboriginal owners of Kuran, murdered by settlers, had been thrown. The boy senses here the smell 'of blood and death . . . something invisible which made the air too potent to breathe . . . some cold and ancient secret of the land itself' (McGahan, 2004: 326) and begins to realise that, should his uncle make him his heir, the ownership of Kuran would prove 'no gift . . . [but] a burden' (McGahan, 2004: 327).

The contrast between him and his uncle is drawn here and the narrative closes on Williams'. Not long after the violent collapse of his movement, McIvor dies in the fire which consumes the decaying mansion, the Kuran homestead—a properly melodramatic ending, of course, in which the 'baddie' is destroyed. For our present purposes, however, it is worth noting that the lurid description of him as a thing of terror also has him turn his head 'slowly, searching, just as it had been searching the first time William had seen it' (McGahan, 2004: 367). Perhaps this is to suggest that the other side of the frontier he has drawn so firmly cannot be denied.

The other work I want to explore—though only briefly—*The Secret River* (Grenville, 2005) takes us into this country, suggesting a positive definition of 'border' not as a place where the other is rejected but where a new exchange may begin. There is also a personal urgency in this novel. Its central character is loosely based on the figure of Grenville's great-great-great-grandfather and had its beginnings at the Walk for Reconciliation across the Harbour Bridge in 2000 when the novelist's eyes met those of an Aboriginal woman who smiled at her. 'In that instant of putting my own ancestor together with this woman's ancestor,' she writes, 'everything swivelled: the country, the place, my sense of myself in it'. Walking across the bridge 'we were strolling towards reconciliation—what I had to do was cross the hard way, through the deep water of our history' (Grenville, 2006: 35).

Reimagining the story of her ancestor, whom she calls William Thornhill, Grenville explores the beginnings of division, attempting to understand rather than to blame. Her ancestor, a poor man transported for life for stealing, belongs to the 'tradition of catastrophe', a victim of the system but also, in the long run, its beneficiary since it enables him to take up land, displacing its Aboriginal owners and finally involving him in a massacre to destroy their resistance. Illiterate and at bay before the strangeness of this place, he has inherited the prejudices of his culture. The novel is not interested in Manichean notions of good and evil, however, but in the way out of the *cul de sac* in which we find ourselves. I can only look briefly at two key scenes

The first tries to sum up what really happened when Thornhill went to the native camp to order them to leave. He invokes English notions of property, telling them: *'This is mine now. Thornhill's place'*. But this is not England, and English law, like the English language means nothing to his hearers and his words flow past them 'as if they mattered as little as a current of air' (Grenville, 2006: 196). As for Thornhill 'the Aboriginal presence is a hollow . . . a space of difference' (Grenville, 2006: 14). Neither side understands the other and so the encounter foreshadows the violence by which the impasse is resolved. 'A conversation had taken place. There had been an inquiry and an answer. But what inquiry, which answer? They stared at each other, their words between them like a wall' (Grenville, 2006: 197). The question then is how the wall *might* be breached so that we will not be swept along, as Thornhill was, by the current of violence.

The novel's conclusion provides a second scene which suggests a possible answer as Thornhill, now an old man, sits at sunset to watch the light on the cliffs opposite blazing gold, even after the dusk had left them 'glowing secretively with an after-light that came from the rocks themselves' (Grenville, 2006: 334). The cliffs are a wall. But something glimmers there in them which, it is implied, will lead him through them into the land itself where he senses still the Aboriginal presence. It is not clear what this may signify. But what seems clear is that now he is at last beginning to be aware of the other. If we accept Levinas' view of the place of the other this may mean the beginning of a properly ethical life and at least a glimpse of the meaning of existence (Hand, 1993: 85).

References

Grenville, Kate, *Searching For The Secret River* (Melbourne: Text Publishing, 2006).

Grenville, Kate, *The Secret River* (Melbourne: Text Publishing, 2005).

Hand, Sean, editor, The Levinas Reader (Oxford: Blackwell, 1993).

McGahan, Andrew, *The White Earth* (Sydney: Allen & Unwin, 2004).

Mellick, JSD, editor, *Portable Australian Authors: Henry Kingsley* (St Lucia: University of Queensland Press, 1982).

Moi, Toril, *Sexual/Textual Politics: Feminist Literary Theory* (London: Routledge, 1991).

Ricoeur, Paul, *The Symbolism Of Evil* (Boston: Beacon Press, 1969).

Susin, Luiz, Carlos, 'A Critique Of The Identity Paradigm', in *Concilium*, 55/2, Summer 2000.

Wentworth, WC, in Turner, Ian, editor, *The Australian Dream* (Melbounre: Sun Books, 1968).

Wright, Judith, The *Generations Of Men* (Melbourne: Oxford University Press, 1965).

6

The Poetics Of Place: Judith Wrigth's 'At Cooloola'

Let us begin by recalling and honouring the land on which we are gathered and the people who lived on and cared for it for thousands of years. This is not a sentimental gesture. DH Lawrence defined sentimentality as 'working off in words of feelings you haven't really got'. But we are concerned here with the reality of place and with our feelings for it, and the fact that it has a history and that its First Peoples have, since time immemorial, been an essential part of it. To acknowledge them therefore is crucial to a proper understanding of it. So I would argue that our failure to do this in the past may be one of the reasons for the crisis in our relations with the land which is now facing us.

Let me elaborate further on this. It helps to explain why we need to develop what I call a 'poetics of place', a feeling for the land and for its First Peoples. Mircea Eliade, for instance, sees this the 'transformation of chaos into cosmos', as the primary task of any people newly arrived in a place hitherto unknown to them' (Eliade, 1974: 10). Yet by and large we have not been very successful in doing this. As Aboriginal leader Patrick Dodson observes; 'most Australians don't know how to think themselves into the country, into the land' whereas Aboriginal people 'find it hard to think without the land' (Keeffe, 2003: 35). The recent controversy over the short-listing for the Archibald Prize of an Aboriginal artist's self-portrait, which was essentially a painting of the country in which the artist lived, is an example of this difference.

In fact, in the past and possibly still in the present, it seems as if many of us feared the land. In the early years of settlement especially, there was much talk of 'conquering' it—conquest, after all, was the dominant concern of colonisation. The first settlers mostly saw the land as an empty container to be filled with animals, crops, towns and cities and so rendered 'productive'. It was, in Paul Carter's words, a kind of theatre in which 'Nature's painted curtains [were] drawn aside to reveal heroic man at his epic labour on the stage of history' (Carter, 1987: xv). But it seems to me that ignoring the power of the land has held back the work which Peter Hay has argued is necessary for any would-be civilised community. That is the creation of a 'moral community', of finding our place in the larger scheme of things, of what Eliade calls the 'cosmos'.

Emmanuel Levinas point that it is when the ego lays down its sovereignty the meaning of being becomes clear (Hand, 1993: 85) is relevant here. What confronted us when we arrived in this country was an other-than-self, an environment very different from anything we had known on the other side of the world. A reminder that there are 'more things in heaven and earth than are dreamed of' in our Western culture, that ultimately we are not in charge of the universe but that we are—to borrow this time from Martin Heidegger —'thrown' into existence as *Dasein,* the point at which Being (*Sein*) knows itself as there (*da*) and mortal and finite. This, as Levinas argues, is the beginning of a genuinely ethical existence which rests on responsibility.

Self is not supreme; instead it is involved in and responsible to being as a whole. It follows therefore that settling in a new country is not so much a matter of exploiting it for our own human ends, *building on* it, as of learning to *dwell in* it, becoming part of a larger reality, what Heidegger calls 'the fourfold', a relationship between 'earth and sky, divinities and mortals' (Heidegger, 1975: 1). Significantly, this is how Aboriginal peoples have always lived in and with this country, though by and large it is not typical of settler societies like ours. In my view, however, the 'Great Silence' which has surrounded Aboriginal people and their culture has lead us to view the land and its history almost exclusively from a 'white' perspective, eliminating 'a whole quadrant' of reality from our understanding (Ley, 2006: 37).

From the beginning, however, one strain of our culture has attempted to explore and celebrate this area of reality, taking up the task of transforming 'chaos into cosmos'. This is the 'poetic' tradition, the area of the arts in general and of poetry in particular. It is concerned with the dimension of the unconscious, of 'the archaic, the oneiric, the nocturnal' which, Paul Ricoeur argues, is accessible only by means of symbols. It is 'the surveyor's staff and guide for becoming oneself' (Ricoeur, 1969: 348), expressing what may otherwise be inexpressible, thus interrogating many of our cultural certainties and opening up new possibilities. This, I suggest, is happening in Judith Wright's poem 'At Cooloola' to which we now turn.

First of all, the poem needs to be put in context. Wright was born into a pastoral family who had lived in and by the land from the first half of the nineteenth century. Unusually, however, she was not entirely at ease with this colonial inheritance, and it was the land which was the source of this unease. As a child it was her constant companion:

> 'As a poet you have to imitate somebody', she wrote, looking back, 'but since . . . I had a beautiful landscape outside that I was in so

much and loved so much . . . it was my main subject from the start . . . It comes to me naturally'. But it also became her teacher and the lessons it taught were often at odds with her culture's: 'Most children are brought up in the "I" tradition these days—the ego, it's me and what I think. But when you live in very close contact with a large and splendid landscape as I did, you feel yourself a good deal smaller than just I' (Brady, 1998: 469).

So the land was not just a background to the self but an active force at work upon and within it, 'full of a deep and urgent meaning' which challenged the colonial culture to which she belonged. 'These hills and plains . . . these rivers and plants and animals . . . contained the hidden depths of a past beyond anything that cities and the British invasion had to offer' (Wright, 1992: 51). Her loyalty lay there in the land, not in the glorification of settlement. So her much quoted poem, 'Bullocky', which is often read as a celebration of the pioneering myth, actually presents him not as a hero but as a madman.

'The hidden depths of the past' which she sensed in the land bespoke a presence which was also an absence for which she was somehow responsible. One of her early poems, 'Bora Ring', for instance, a reflection on the remains of an Aboriginal ceremonial site, is about this presence:

> The hunter is gone: the spear
> is splintered underground; the painted bodies
> a dream the world breathed sleeping and forgot.
> The nomad feet are still.

But the responsibility remains. Their absence speaks 'an unsaid word', an accusation

> that fastens in the blood the ancient curse,
> the fear as old as Cain (Wright, 1994: 8).

In this world view we are all responsible for and to one another and to the land as living presence.

In this way she dissents from her inheritance. 'For A Pastoral Family', written in the 1980s reflects on the imperial assumptions of her forbears,

> ... men and women
> who took over as if by right a century and a half
> in an ancient difficult bush. And after all
> the previous owners put up little fight,
> did not believe in ownership, and so were scarcely human

This inheritance, she finds, is an ambiguous 'base for poetry/a doubtful song that has a dying fall' (Wright, 1994: 406), rejecting its implicit assumption that might equals right, that accepts the inevitability of Aboriginal dispossession and the logic of the imperial history which has or less obliterated the Aboriginal story. This was exemplified by the judgment in the case of the Yorta Yorta people in Victoria which argued that 'the tides of history' had flowed over their land and abolished any claim they might have had to it.

Wright's feeling for the land, however, took her beyond this kind of history to the time of the earth which had a different kind of story to tell. Another early poem, 'Nigger's Leap, New England', (Wright, 1994: 15–16) is about this story. It is a meditation on a place not far from where she grew up. In the nineteenth century, Aboriginal people were driven over a cliff in retribution for spearing some of the settlers' cattle. But the power of place continued to speak accusingly:

> Did we not know their blood [that] channelled our rivers,
> and the black dust our crops ate was their dust.
>
> As far as the earth is concerned 'all men are one
> man at last' and those who died here are 'ourselves
> writ strange'. So . . . [w]e should have known the night
> that tided up the cliffs and hid them had the same
> question on its tongue for us.

This awareness contrasts with the complacency which lead one critic to write that the poem 'has for its subject . . . the suicide of the Aboriginals years ago' (Brissenden, 1968: 42). As the use of the adjective 'Aboriginals' rather the noun, 'Aborigines' suggests, he sees them collectively merely as part of a category different from his own and, as the word 'suicide' implies, somehow morally deficient. He is unable to think outside his ethnocentric frame and to acknowledge the claims of the other. It is the same inability evident in those who reject what they dismiss as 'the Black Armband school of history', which attempts to see things from the point of view of those excluded from official history.

In the poem, 'At Coolola' (Wright, 1994: 140–1), Wright explores the link between Aboriginal people and the land and the ways in which white settlement interrupted it. But she also acknow-ledges her own involvement through her family in this interruption, the way in which, as Levinas puts it, the *'da* of her *Dasein* ' has involved the 'usurpation of somebody else's place' (Hand, 1993: 85). Once again, this poem is a meditation on place which offers a challenge rather than consolation, a demand which she cannot fully meet but cannot avoid. It is set this time in a coastal area of Queensland, Cooloola, an area incidentally where clashes were later to occur between environmentalists and developers intent on exploiting the mineral sands to be found there.

It is evening and the poet is watching a blue crane fishing in a pool. But once again we are drawn into the time of the earth in the realisation that the crane and his kind have been fishing in this pool 'longer than our centuries'. He is therefore 'the certain heir of lake and evening' and he will 'wear their colour till he dies'. But she is a mere onlooker, 'stranger, come of a conquering people'.

The sight of a piece of driftwood shaped like a spear thrust from the pool is a reminder of this, recalling an incident from her grandfather's diary, when one day riding at noon 'a black accoutred warrior armed for fighting' suddenly appeared before him and just as suddenly disappeared. In her family history, *The Generations Of Men,* Wright associates this apparition with an incident some weeks earlier when he had come upon the bodies of three young Aboriginal warriors and one old man lying in the bush, evidently murdered. But he realised that they had been on a peaceful hunting trip since they were not wearing the feathers and clay decorations of men going to war. They had been shot and dragged into the bush, and their bodies half-hidden by branches, perhaps the night before (Wright, 1965: 50). As the local justice of the peace it was his obligation to investigate their deaths. But in fact he had done nothing.

The implication in the poem, however, is that the apparition is a ghost representing the dead, an accusatory ghost since, according to his grand daughter, the killings had remained 'a heavy load' on his conscience. Even today she feels this load as his descendant as she watches the bird fishing in the pool:

> I cannot share his calm, who watch his lake,
> being unloved by all my eyes delight in,

and made uneasy for an old murder's sake.

Ghosts, of course, have no place in current commonsense. But Aboriginal culture did afford them place, and still does: and the poem pays tribute to their beliefs:

> Those Aboriginal people who first named Cooloola
> knew that no land is lost or won by wars,
> for earth is spirit: the invader's feet will tangle
> in nets there and his blood be thinned by fears.

This is the crux of the poem but also of Wright's understanding of place.

It is possible to dismiss this as merely 'poetic'. But many contemporary scientists, increasingly interested in and respectful of the unseen, suggest that the universe may be more open, subtle and supple than we have imagined (Harris, 1998: 9). Some would even regard the cosmos as a 'psychophysical entity' evolving towards increasing consciousness, 'in this way both [producing] us and, ultimately, [participating] in us to become real' (Studer, 1998: 21–2). If this is so the poetic imagination may be more illuminating than 'commonsense'.

Wright was aware of this, writing to a friend that 'even scientists . . . [no] longer regard the physical and the psychic as separate, and all the work being done seems to confirm this—what is the observer, what the observed? Can you tell the dancer from the dance?'(Brady, 1998: 287). It may therefore be true to say, to quote Heidegger, that 'the oldest of the old follows behind us in our thinking and yet it comes to meet us in our thinking' (Heidegger, 1975: 10), and that the land may therefore be haunted. The fear expressed in 'At Cooloola' may be justified therefore. At the same time it may mark a new beginning if, as Levinas suggests, the fear occasioned by the death of others, represents not 'an *individual's* taking fright' (Hand, 1993: 84), but the beginning of genuine moral community, an answer to the appeal of the other—the Aboriginal people and the land being two sides of the one reality here.

If this is so, 'At Cooloola' may have important things to say about the problems facing us at the moment, in the attempt to build and preserve 'moral community', to contest what Hannah Arendt calls the 'catastrophic interiority of the selfish I' (Kristeva, 2001: 39).

To think oneself into the country may therefore be to think oneself into the meaning of being, to 'return to the interiority of non-intentional consciousness . . . to its capacity to fear injustice more than death . . . and to prefer that which justifies being over that which assures it' (Hand, 1993: 85). That, the penultimate stanza of 'At Cooloola' suggests, remains a task yet to be completed by us in this country. But the land itself keeps it before us:

> White shores of sand, plumed reed and paperbark,
> clear heavenly levels frequented by crane and swan—
> I know that we are justified only by love,
> but, oppressed by arrogant guilt, have room for none.

References

Brady, Veronica, *South Of My Days: A Biography Of Judith Wright* (Sydney: Angus & Robertson, 1998).

Brissenden, RF, 'The Poetry of Judith Wright', in Thompson, AV, *Critical Essays On Judith Wright* (Brisbane: Jacaranda Press, 1968).

Carter, Paul, *The Road To Botany Bay: An Essay In Spatial History* (London: Faber & Faber, 1987).

Eliade, Mircea, *The Myth Of The Eternal Return: Or, Cosmos And History* (Princeton: Princeton University Press, 1974).

Hand, Sean, editor, *The Levinas Reader* (Oxford: Blackwell, 1993).

Harris, Lyndon, 'Divine Action: An Interview With John Polkinghorne', in *Cross Currents*, 48/1, Spring 1998.

Heidegger, Martin, 'Building Dwelling Thinking', in *Poetry, Language, Thought* (New York: Harper Colophon Books, 1975).

Keeffe, Kevin, *Paddy's Road: Life Stories Of Patrick Dodson* (Canberra: Aboriginal Studies Press, 2003).

Kristeva, Julia, *Hannah Arendt: Life Is A Narrative* (Toronto: University of Toronto Press, 2001).

Ley, James, '"How Small The Lights Of Home": Andrew Mc Gahan And The Politics Of Guilt', in *Australian Book Review*, 280, April 2006.

Ricoeur, Paul, *The Symbolism Of Evil* (Boston: Beacon Press, 1969).

Studer, James, 'Consciousness And Reality: Our Entry Into Creation', in *Cross Currents*, 48/1, Spring 1998.

Wright, Judith, *Generations Of Men* (Melbourne: Oxford University Press, 1965).

Wright, Judith, *Collected Poems: 1942–1985* (Sydney: Angus & Robertson, 1994).

Wright, Judith, *Going On Talking* (Sydney: Butterfly Books, 1992).

7

An Incident In The Culture Wars: Judith Wright's 'Haunted Land'

We begin with a passage from Judith Wright's family history *The Generations Of Men*, in which she imagines her grandfather, Albert Wright, one of the early settlers on the New England tableland. He is reflecting on the fate of the Aboriginal people who had been a flourishing and dignified community when he and his family had arrived but were now reduced to a diseased and bedraggled minority. Surprisingly, however, Wright has him suspect that he and his fellow newcomers had also been damaged in the encounter, imagining their 'whole civilisation haunted, like a house haunted by the ghost of a dead man buried under it' but also 'by [a] deep and festering consciousness of guilt in themselves' (Wright, 1965: 163). This is evidently a 'Black Armband' approach to history. But before considering the issues this raises, we need to define what is meant by the word 'Australia' and to what extent it can be seen as a 'thinking society and culture'.

I begin by seeing the two as more or less synonymous. If a nation is defined as an 'imagined community', it is an ideological construct. I want to suggest that there may be serious flaws in the way in which we have imagined ourselves, pointing to the limitations of cultural premises underlying this nation which are those of the Enlightenment and the attempts to impose European hegemony that grew out of it. I find an essay by a Brazilian sociologist, Luiz Carlos Susin, illuminating here. He argues that the identity thus generated rests on the story of Ulysses who left home and travelled through strange places intending to return home again or to conquering these places and make them like home. In effect then this story describes 'a closed circle around sameness' (Susin, 2000: 87) from within which the self sallies forth to conquer difference, 'distinguishing and identifying good and evil in a very particular way, based on itself, on its glorious position as basis and referent of the whole of reality spread out at its feet' (Susin, 2000: 80).

I think this is a reasonably accurate description of Australia today. But it goes back to the beginnings of settlement, to settlers like WC Wentworth, for instance, who declared his intention to build 'A new Britannia in another world' (Turner, 1968: 12). The architecture of nineteenth century cities, Melbourne especially, witness to a similar attempt. But such an identity set up a disjunction between the self and its actual environment and signalled a determination to destroy that difference and to remake the environment in the image of our desires. So, drawing on accounts of the arrival of the First Fleet, Paul Carter argues that place figured in them 'simply [as] a stage where history occurred' and that this history was in effect 'a theatrical performance . . . a fabric of self-reinforcing illusions' and the land was a kind of stage on which 'Nature's painted curtains [were] drawn aside to reveal heroic man at his epic labour on the stage of history' (Carter, 1988: xiv–xv).

This refusal to deal with difference is central to Patrick White's novel, *Voss*. His meditation on the myth of the explorer draws a contrast between the Bonners and their circle who cling to the fringes of the self, shrinking from 'the deep end of the unconscious' as they shrink from the interior of the continent and Voss and his party who respond to the challenge of the interior. I would also suggest that it is evident today and that a society deeply suspicious of difference is not likely to be a thinking society or culture. The unfolding twenty-first century may be even more out of touch with reality and problematic than it is today. But it is not the only model of identity. Susin offers an alternative model which is open rather than closed. It is based on the figure of Abraham who left his familiar world and culture in response to a 'call to go further', to move across the known horizon. But it should also be noted that this model implies a return to an ontology and epistemology which gives credence to realities beyond those which are rational, material and measurable. It also supports Mircea Eliade's proposition that the primary task of a people, newly arrived in a country hitherto unknown to them, is metaphysical rather than merely economic, it requires the 'transformation of chaos into 'cosmos' (Eliade, 1974: 10), to find their place there in some larger scheme of things.

A strain running through our literary and artistic culture has pursued this task from the beginnings, often against the grain of the larger culture which has been largely dominated by neo-Darwinian and neo-Utilitarian modes of thinking and feeling. Where this culture was largely intent on dominating the land and making it serve our purposes and ignoring the wisdom of its First Peoples, this strain tended to see the land more as a metaphysical than as an economic resource. In *Such Is Life*, for instance, Joseph Furphy's Tom Collins declares that 'the Australian attains full consciousness of his own nationality' in the interior, seeing the land itself which he sees as anything but subservient to our intentions but as 'grave, subdued, self-centred', an other which demands respect but which also contains 'a latent meaning' to be 'faithfully and lovingly interpreted' (Barnes, 1981: 65). Many subsequent writers, artists and musicians have made similar suggestions, though there is no time to explore their work here.

Instead, let us return to Judith Wright since she brings together a number of factors necessary for the formation of a thinking culture and society by connecting literary concerns with political, historical, sociological and even economic issues. It is true, therefore, that the passage we have been discussing could be said to belong to a 'Black Armband' school of history. It also enables us to situate the 'History Wars' in a more wide-ranging and, therefore, more intellectually respectable context, seeing it as a clash between two different world views and thus of ideas of national identity.

As Wright describes her grandfather, he is in fact torn between these two world views. Aware, on the one hand, that he is one of the conquerors who displaced the land's Aboriginal owners and were destroying their culture, but, on the other hand, feeling a 'queer sympathy' with one of them. This was the old black fellow, Paddy, one of his workers, and the culture which enabled him to 'answer his moods with an understanding [he] seldom found among white men, who, intent on their own interests and problems, took little notice of the needs of other people' (Wright, 1965: 159). Unlike many of his contemporaries, however, Albert Wright is troubled by this sensitivity and does not see it as a sign of inferiority. Rather it makes him question his own culture which, in its pursuit of 'money, security, prosperity', in 'a whirlwind of destruction', seems to him to be 'speaking words of power, but not words of life' (Wright, 1965: 161).

Here Wright is interrogating the founding story of our identity which is 'the permanent secret of [our] meaning and obligation' (Susin, 2000: 81). To the extent that in it the self alone is the arbiter of good and evil and acknowledges no authority beyond it, it could be seen as ethically deficient. At least this is so if one accepts Emmanuel Levinas' proposition that it is only 'in the laying down by the ego of its sovereignty . . . that we find ethics and also perhaps the very spirituality of the soul, but most certainly the question of the meaning of being, that is, its appeal for justification' (Hand, 1993: 85). Moreover, in this view justification does not depend upon some abstract and anonymous law, or judicial entity, 'but by the extent to which one is aware of and acts upon one's responsibility for the other' (Hand, 1993: 82), for other human beings, but also for the natural world on which we depend.

This takes us back to the Abrahamic model of identity which is open and responsive to the other and moves out of the 'closed circle around sameness' towards it. In refusing to do this, as Wright argues, we have suffered a 'mortal wound . . . a deep and festering consciousness of guilt'. In turn, the anxiety and pain it caused has fuelled the 'hatred and contempt that so many . . . held for the blacks' which is often used to justify our treatment of them. Until it is dealt with, she believed, it 'would remain forever at the root of this country, making every achievement empty and every struggle vain' (Wright, 1965: 163).

This is not the kind of argument most of us are accustomed to conduct. But it is not to say that it may not be worth doing so. Reflecting over the debates which followed the High Court's Mabo judgement, Raimond Gaita makes this point: 'One should not, as critics of Mabo tend to do, restrict the concept of national interest to economic interests or to the interest of having an undivided body politic . . . Even in politics, we are, inescapably, moral beings' (Gaita, 2000: 278). All of us are ultimately responsible for and to one another. As John Donne famously put it, no one is an island but each of us is part of the one great continent of life.

Once more, it is worth returning to the original experience of settlement in which, to put it simply, perhaps over-simply, we attempted to impose time, the linear time of imperial history, on place. The fact that the land and its First Peoples resisted only intensified our determination to assert our mastery and our rebellion against any authority outside the self. As Ian Turner observed:

> These new Australians were involved with moulding an untouched and often intransigent environment to their will. A religion which was appropriate for the ordered society and regular living of rural England seemed irrelevant to pioneering labour in the Australian bush. Men carved their own lives out of a remote and monstrously difficult wilderness; what they achieved, they owed to themselves, and they found little for which to thank their fathers' heaven (Turner, 1968: x).

To draw on the taxonymy developed by Helene Cixous (Moi, 1991: 110–3), this is an essentially 'masculine' position within the 'economy of the proper' which is concerned with property, propriety and appropriation. It thus circles around itself and is suspicious of the other, assuming that 'the moment you receive something you are effectively "open" to the other, and . . . you have only one wish . . . hastily to return the gift, to break the circuit of an exchange that could have no end . . . to be nobody's child, to owe no one a thing' (Moi, 1991: 112). In contrast, the 'feminine', the 'economy of the gift', echoes the story of Abraham since it gives to and receives from the other, moving across boundaries and being open to new understandings and attentive to the 'resonance of fore-language . . . the language of 1,000 tongues which knows neither enclosure nor death' (Moi, 1991: 113).

This is the way Wright, and indeed many others like her, lived. As a child she spent a good deal of time alone exploring the family property. As she put it later: 'Most children are . . . brought up in the "I" tradition these days—the ego, it's me and what I think. But when you live in very close contact with a large and splendid landscape you feel yourself a good deal smaller than just I' (Brady, 1998: 469). For her the land was not just an empty space to be filled with crops and animals but a living presence in which she sensed a story which interrogated that of her own people and history.

'Bora Ring', one of her early poems, is a good example not only of her sense of this presence but also of the claims it makes, opening with a sense that their

> . . . song is gone; the dance
> is secret with the dancers in the earth,
> the ritual useless, and the tribal story
> lost in an alien tale—

but concluding with an acceptance of responsibility for this loss as:

> . . . the rider's heart
> halts at a sightless shadow, and unsaid word
> that fastens in the blood the ancient curse,
> the fear as old as Cain (Wright, 1994: 8).

This brings us to the crux of the argument over 'Black Armband' history, the charge that it is the product of bleeding hearts rather than intelligent minds.

I would contend that this kind of acceptance of responsibility for past events is more hard-headed than the guilt which actually underlies this charge. If we accept Paul Ricoeur's definition of guilt as 'feeling responsible for not being responsible' (Ricoeur, 1969: 21), it is a definition which suggests its links with the anxieties and over-reaction evident in our dealings with Aboriginal Australia.

Wright does this in one of her later poems, 'The Dark Ones' (Wright, 1994: 354–5). It is set in a typical country town on pension day, the day when Aboriginal fringe-dwellers, otherwise invisible, come to town to collect their govern-ment hand-outs. The poem's focus is on the whites' reaction to this appearance, first of all on their anxiety and then on its source. She implies that for the whites, the Aborigines represent the shadow side of the self, its negative aspect, 'the sum of all the unpleasant qualities we like to hide, together with the insufficiently developed functions and the contents of the personal unconscious':

> On the other side of the road
> the dark ones stand.
> Something leaks in our blood
> like the ooze from a wound (Storr, 1983: 87).

The poem goes on to suggest the way in which the continuing existence of the Aborigines challenges the sense of self which depends on the imperial story: the whites figure as the spearhead of the evolution which, at the other end of its scale, has doomed Aborigines to give way before them and die out:

> A shudder like breath caught
> runs through the town.
> Are *they* still here? We thought . . .
> Let us alone.

This identity, as we have been arguing, takes no responsibility for anyone or anything other than the self and its interests. Against such an identity Raimond Gaita quotes Martin Buber: 'The idea of responsibility needs to be brought back from the province of a specialised ethics; of an "ought" that swings free in the air, into that of real life. Genuine responsibility exists only when there is real responding' (Gaita, 2000: 284). The definition of 'real life' is implicit in Gaita's further point that the story by which we make sense of our lives should exist 'against the background of compassionate responsiveness to the defining vulnerability of a common human condition' (Gaita, 2000: 282). A thinking society and thinking culture, which will enable us to negotiate the challenging future ahead, needs to take this into account.

References

Barnes, John, editor, *Portable Australian Authors: Joseph Furphy* (St Lucia: Queensland University Press, 1981).

Carter, Paul, *The Road To Botany Bay* (London: Faber & Faber, 1988).

Eliade, Mircea, *The Myth Of The Eternal Return* (Princeton: Princeton University Press, 1974).

Gaita, Raimond, 'Guilt, Shame and Collective Responsibility', in Michelle Grattan, editor, *Essays On Australian Reconciliation* (Melbourne: Black Inc, 2000).

Hand, Sean, editor, *The Levinas Reader* (Oxford: Blackwell, 1993).

Moi, Toril, *Sexual/Textual Politics: Feminist Literary Theory* (London: Routledge, 1991).

Storr, Anthony, *Jung: Selected Writings* (London: Fontana Press, 1983).

Susin, Luiz Carlos, 'A Critique Of The Identity Paradigm', in *Concilium*, 55/2, Summer 2000.

Turner, Ian, editor, *The Australian Dream* (Melbourne: Sun Books, 1968).

White, Patrick, *Flaws In The Glass* (London: Cape, 1981).

Wright, Judith, *The Generations Of Men* (Melbourne: Oxford University Press, 1965).

8

Blasphemy And Sacrilege In The Arts: The Challenge Of Kim Scott's *Benang*

We are engaged in an unfashionable discussion. The dictionary defines blasphemy and sacrilege as profane talk or action, an offence against what is sacred. Rudolph Otto calls the sacred that *mysterium terribile, tremendum et fascinans* at the heart of existence to which we owe reverence and obedience (Otto, 1923: 4). But the West in general today and Australian society in particular seems to have little sense of this kind of reality. If anything, the tendency that AG Stephens identified in 1905 has intensified. He wrote that 'there is in the developing Australian character a sceptical and utilitarian spirit that values the present hour and refuses to sacrifice the present for any visionary future lacking a rational guarantee' (Turner, 1968: x). Technology, which seems to allow us to dominate and control the world, has intensified this refusal so that, lacking a centre outside the self and its desires, we exist in a state of 'pure circulation [in which] . . . there is no point of reference . . . and value radiates in all directions . . . without reference to anything whatsoever' (Baudrillard, 1993: 5).

There are some who would regard the growth of religious fundamentalism as a return to the sacred. But the sacred as we have defined it is a power which stands over against the self, though it may speak to and within it, whereas fundamentalism is grounded in the self, in its desires for power and esteem, for example, or for certainty and security. If this is so, the notion of blasphemy and sacrilege challenges current notions of reality and value. Yet I would argue that a culture which lacks a sense of the sacred, of a mystery beyond the self which constitutes what Kierkegaard calls an 'Archimedean point' of existence, is in many ways deficient and destructive because it is at odds with what is ultimately the case. For most traditional cultures, this Archimedean point has long been established and is culturally accepted, though, whether or not it is acted, upon is another matter. But for settler societies like ours it needs to be discovered anew. So Mircea Eliade argues that the 'transformation of chaos into cosmos' is the primary task and more important than economic or material development (Eliade, 1974: 10). Arguably, however, by and large this task is still incomplete in Australia, largely for historical reasons. Ours is a society which is the product of the imperial history on to which, Karl Jaspers suggests, there has been 'loaded a grandeur . . . stolen from God' (Kohler, 1992: 145). In effect, it is based on the story of Ulysses, who left home and traveled through strange places but always with the intention of returning home or of turning these places into the equivalent of home (Susin, 2002: 87), making 'a new Britannia in another world', as one of the early settlers put it (Wentworth, 1969, 12). But this is to reject difference, to seek to destroy or assimilate it, establishing in effect a 'closed circle around sameness' (Susin, 2002: 87).

Its notion of good and evil, which according to Levinas constitutes the 'first philosophy' (Hand, 1993: 82) is, however, limited since, as Luiz Carlos Susin argues, it defines good and evil 'in a very particular way based on itself, on its glorious position as basis and referent of all of reality spread out at its feet' (Susin, 2002: 80). The result is that it has little or no ability to relate to, much less feel for, the other/Other. Dirk Moses makes this point in his review of

Bain Attwood's *Telling The Truth About Aboriginal History: a priori*, settler Australians have no reason to care about indigenous experiences. Even if they acknowledge Aboriginal suffering, they engage in a simple moral calculus . . . any injustice that has been committed is redeemed by the just nature of the modern society that replaced the indigenous ones (Moses, 2005: 14).

The parallel between this passage and what Hannah Arendt has to say about Germany in the 1930s, however, is troubling. In Hitler's Germany, many people were no longer able to recognise evil and it had lost what she called the 'quality of temptation'. Many, she writes ironically, 'must have been tempted not to murder, not to rob, not to let their neighbours go off to their doom, and not to become accomplices in all these crimes by benefiting from them. But, God knows, they had learned to resist temptation' (Arendt, 1994: 150). The ethical and the ontological are two sides of the one reality since, as Levinas says we recognise the other as resembling us but also as being unlike us. So in effect it is the relationship with the other which makes us properly human, that is, open and compassionate.

Returning to Dirk Moses, this understanding seems to me implicit when he writes that, if settler Australians are to get outside the moral calculus which prevents them from feeling for and with Aboriginal Australians, then 'they need to be moved by stories of [their plight] and believe them to be true'. Similarly, 'if historians are to promote moral consciousness . . . regarding the value of alterity, they need to master a certain rhetoric and emotional register . . . rather than engage in theoretical parlour games' (Moses, 2005: 14). That is why the arts may have an important part to play. They challenge matter-of-fact by offering new possibilities and injecting 'a core of meaning beneath the platitude of immediate physical presence' (Levy, 1998: 16) or of the frame of our present culture. As Sir Philip Sidney argued, in his 'Apology For Poetry', other forms of knowledge more or less deal with what is already the case. Only poetry, by which he means the arts in general, 'disdaining to be tied to any such subjection . . . doth grow in effect another nature, in making things either better . . . or quite anew' (Abrams, 1962: 426), and takes us beyond the 'closed circle around sameness', enabling us to feel for and with the other.

Let us turn then to a recent work of fiction, Kim Scott's novel *Benang*, which does that, it gives an account of the story of the settlement of south eastern Western Australia through the eyes of its Aboriginal inhabitants. Significantly, however, Scott himself has a foot in both camps, having been brought up as part of mainstream white society but having discovered recently that he is a descendant of the Nyoongar people of the area. His central character and the novel's narrator, Harley, who tells the Nyoongar story, is also exploring his own newly discovered identity. But he is also interrogating ours as well. He is the 'first-born-successfully-white-man-in-the-family-line' (Scott, 1999: 22), the result of his grandfather's belief that the only way to survive is to 'breed out' their 'blackness' and turn his descendants into whites. But he also functions as our mirror image, 'an imaginary figure' who causes us 'to be [ourselves] while at the same time never seeming like [ourselves]' (Scott, 1999: 19), and thus involves us in the story of settlement seen from the other side of the frontier.

It is a grim story of dispossession, murders, rapes, imprisonment and humiliation. It interrogates and, in a sense, blasphemes against the pieties of the official history of settlement, setting it in the context of personal experience and suggesting that historical events cannot be justified by 'referring to some abstract and anonymous law' or supposed divine or historical sanction but must be judged by its effect on others. Judged in this way, it appears that our 'place in the sun', our possession of this country meant, as Levinas puts it, writing of recent Western culture generally, 'the usurpation of spaces belonging to the other . . . whom [we] have . . . oppressed or starved, or driven out into a third world' (Hand, 1993: 83).

This dispossession is *Benang's* subject. Its ethical basis, however, reaches beyond imperial history which rests on material success or failure, towards an ethic of responsibility. The assumption is that, in the larger scheme of things, the meaning of human existence does not depend only on the 'winners' and that the 'losers', the dead, those who, already vanquished and forgotten, may have a meaning yet to be realised. This makes *Benang* an uncomfortable book since it breaks the taboo, the defence against the 'peril of the soul . . . in the presence of things that are forbidden to profane experience [and] . . . cannot be approached without risk when one is not ritually prepared' (Ricoeur, 1969: 21), which protects us from awareness of the Aboriginal side of our history.

But the novel is also doubly blasphemous since it questions our cherished notions of reality. Harley is a figure of fantasy, as well as of history, and thus exists on a 'level in which simultaneous estrangement from himself and intimacy with himself are played out' (Scott, 1999: 23)—something which mocks our monolithic sense of identity. He also parodies the identity imposed on him as an Aborigine, remarking early in his story that '[i]t was terrible to see the shapes, the selves, I took': now a romantic figure, 'motionless against a setting sun; posture perfect, brow noble, features fine'; now a drunk, 'slumped, grinning, furrow-browed, with a bottle in my hand'; now a cowboy or boxer or footballer, or a 'tiny figure, sprawled on the ground in some desert place, dying' (Scott, 1999: 14). This, of course, points to the ways in which we refuse to allow others their own identity but impose our perceptions on them.

The novel also attacks the policy of assimilation, of taking children away from their families, trying to destroy their culture and so on, which was justified by the claim that it was intended, in the words of AO Neville, Chief Protector of Aborigines in Western Australia, to 'uplift and elevate these people to our own plane'. Harley parodies this rationale by claiming to have a remarkable 'propensity for elevation', a tendency to float upwards, which he constantly does, both indoors and outdoors. This parody, however, has a serious intention. One passage especially indicates the blasphemous nature of this project, the way in which people were robbed of their identity and dignity and turned into mere objects of manipulation. It shows Harley's grandfather, Ern, and Sergeant Hall, the local policeman and thus the official 'Protector of Aborigines', discussing Ern's suggestion that Hall might marry one of the women in Ern's family:

> They spoke of breeding and uplifting. These two hairy angels wished to seize people in their long arms and haul them to their own level. Their minds held flickering images of canvas Ascensions, with fat, pale cherubs, spiralling upwards, into the light. They saw steps leading up stone pyramids, and realised that some creatures were simply unable to continue higher, though the steps were there for them. Their noble selves sat at the top . . . Those hairy angels, scratching at their groins. Belching. Drinking beer (Scott, 1999: 77).

The irreverence is devastating, and it targets notions of racial superiority. But the trope of elevation also echoes a notion of the sacred common to many indigenous peoples, in the image of magical flight which is associated with the comprehension of secret sacred things and expresses the belief that some transformation, even some ontological mutation, has occurred in the person him/herself (Scott, 1999: 24). Seen in this light, Harley's propensity could also be taken as a critique of the superficial weightlessness and decentredness of Western culture and an assertion of belief in the sacred. Certainly for him there is nothing sacred about the imperial story. It is merely a 'bad smell' not only of the Aboriginal dead but also of the 'anxiety, of anger and betrayal' which followed.

This story, then, ignores 'otherworldly' ideas of the ethical, calling us instead to respond to the claims these others whose faces summon and call us into question. To the extent that we settlers are unable to recognise that there is an 'other' at the heart of ourselves, *Benang* challenges us to see ourselves and others through the eyes of these others.

This is clear in the scene in which the police capture an Aborigine and hang him under the approving eyes of a group of settlers while, from the reserve, his own people, a 'little troupe', watch helplessly in the gathering dusk. The doubling effect works powerfully here. For once noticing the black onlookers, the whites, we are told, regard them as a 'circus . . . A zoo. A bloody freak show' despising the poverty of the reserve to which they have been condemned, 'a few rough shelters and a small house and stable' (Scott, 1999: 332). The drift of the passage and of the novel as a whole, however, suggests that what they are seeing is in fact the mirror image of themselves and their culture, a shadow which haunts them.

So far, it seems as if the novel's approach is merely negative, a story of suffering and defeat. But there is also a positive aspect, implicit in the title: 'Benang' means 'tomorrow' and it is the last word of the novel's final sentence: 'We are still here, Benang' (Scott, 1999: 497). The 'closed circle around sameness' of imperial culture, its 'totalisation of identity' will break up as the novel points to the life of the land itself and thus to a larger, more enduring sense of reality and value than that of our culture intent on domination, possession and control.

Once more Judith Wright helps us understand what is at issue here, when she reflects that in effect, when we arrived, the Aborigines said to us newcomers: 'you must understand us or you must kill us'. They were unable to give up a culture and their identity because it bound them irrevocably, not merely to a specific place or time, but also to the life of the cosmos. But for the settlers this 'understanding would have meant some renunciation impossible to be made' (Wright, 1965: 163). It asked them to surrender the exclusive power and possessions they claimed for themselves and acknowledge a power beyond themselves, the power of the sacred.

Because the Aboriginal peoples have made this acknowledgement, *Benang* suggests, in the long run, they will survive, in tune with the cosmos rather than with history. It is this attunement which, despite the grim story he has to tell, sustains Harley. For most of us the land is merely an empty stage on which to play out our dreams of power and possession. But for him and his people it is a living presence which speaks to and through him, something he has not lost, even if he has become the 'first white man born'. So his self is not solitary, nor is the story he has to tell: '[I]t is not really *me* who sings, for . . . through me we hear the rhythm of many feet pounding the earth, and the strong pulse of countless hearts beating' (Scott, 1999: 9), listening to 'the creak and rustle of various plants in various winds, the countless beatings of different wings, the many strange and musical calls of animals who have come from this place right here' (Scott, 1999: 9–10).

That is why, despite everything, *Benang* concludes on a triumphant note:

> Speaking from the heart I tell you I am part of a much older story, one of a perpetual billowing from the sea, with its rhythms of return, return, and remain. Even now we gather, on chilly evenings, sometimes only a very few of us, sometimes more. We gather our strength in this way. From the heart of all of us. Pale, burnt and shrivel-led, I hover in the campfire smoke and sing as best I can. I am not alone (Scott, 1999: 497).

The colonial self is monolithic. But the indigenous culture it attempts to overcome is multiple and in that sense indestructible. So the novel ends with a challenge which is also partly a threat:

> I offer these words, especially to those of you I embarrass, and who turn away from the shame of seeing me; or perhaps it is because your eyes smart as the wind blows the smoke a little towards you, and you hear something like a million million many-sized hearts beating, and the whispering of waves, leaves, grasses. We are still here, Benang (Scott, 1999: 497).

Seen from this point of view, contemporary Australian culture can be seen as blasphemous. For in a sacred culture the world is not the creation of human history or technology but of unseen presences with whom we cooperate. Reality therefore is not closed in on itself. Everything holds together in a system of correspondences and resonances.

References

Arendt, Hannah, *Eichmann In Jerusalem: A Report On The Banality Of Evil* (Camberwell: Penguin, 1994).

Abrams, MH, et al, editors, *The Norton Anthology Of English Literature*, I. 9 (New York: WW Norton, 1962).

Baudrillard, Jean, *The Transparency Of Evil*, translated by James Benedict (London: Verso, 1993).

Hand, Sean, editor, *The Levinas Reader* (Oxford: Blackwell, 1993).

Katz, Claire Elise, 'The Problem Of Evil And The Question Of Responsibility', in *Cross Currents*, 55/2, Summer 2005.

Kohler, Lotte and Hans Saner, Hans, editor, *Correspondence Hannah Arendt Karl Jaspers 1926–1969* (New York: Harcourt Brace, 1992).

Levy, Pierre, *Becoming Virtual: Reality In The Digital Age* (New York: Plenum Trade, 1998).

Metz, Johann Baptist, *Faith In History And Society* (New York: Seabury Press, 1980).

Mircea, Eliade, *Symbolism* (New York: Crossroad, 1990).

Moses, A Dirk, 'Provincialism', in *Australian Book Review*, Number 276, November 2005.

Otto, Rudolph, *The Idea Of The Holy* (Oxford: Oxford University Press, 1923).

Ricoeur, Paul, *The Symbolism Of Evil* (Boston: Beacon Press, 1969).

Scott, Kim *Benanag* (Fremantle: Fremantle Arts Centre Press, 1999).

Susin, Luiz Carlos, 'A Critique Of The Identity Paradigm', in *Concilium*, 55/2, Summer 2002.

Turner, Ian, editor, *The Australian Dream* (Melbourne: Sun Books, 1969).

Wentworth, William Charles, in Ian Turner, editor, *The Australian Dream* (Melbourne: Sun Books, 1969).

Wright, Judith, *The Generations Of Men* (Melbourne: Oxford University Press, 1965).

9

After Cronulla: The Defense of *The White Earth*

Violence, culture and identity are closely bound in a settler society like Australia. According to Deborah Bird Rose, the space we inhabit is 'wounded'; most of us are marked by the 'epistemic violence' (Gayatri Spivak) of colonisation. This, I suggest, was evident at the Cronulla riots of a few years back. But assertions of this kind are difficult to explore, belonging as they do to the unconscious, the dimension of 'the archaic, the nocturnal, the oneiric. (Ricoeur, 1969: 34). But symbols, 'the surveyor's staff and guide for 'becoming oneself' (Ricoeur, 1969: 13), and also the stuff of fiction, may provide some access to deepen our understanding. So let me base my argument on an exploration of Andrew McGahan's 1995 Miles Franklin award winning novel, *The White Earth* (McGahan, 2004).

According to the author, the book expresses a premonition that Australia is 'on the verge of something very dark and ugly politically' (Ley, 2006: 35)—which perhaps is what surfaced during the Cronulla riots. The novel's tone is Gothic, full of images of decay and excess centred on a decaying mansion, a kind of fortress in which its ageing megalomaniac owner, John McIvor, attempts to 'hold his beliefs against the world' (Ley, 2006: 38)—recall, if you like, the Fortress Australia mentality of the previous Howard government. But where the lines between good and evil are usually clearly drawn in melodrama, it is more ambiguous here since the story is filtered through the confusedly impressionable eyes of McIvor's nephew William—suggesting a more general crisis of value within the culture as a whole. William's ineffectual father has died in an accident and his mother is a figure of angry weakness so that the boy is dependent on the rich uncle who wants to indoctrinate him with his values. As James Ley notes, therefore, William is a figure of *anomie* who finds himself in a situation he can neither understand nor control and lacks the ability and will to remove himself, allowing himself to be carried uneasily along by events (Ley, 2006: 35). Perhaps there is a parallel between him and many of the participants in the events at Cronulla, so unsure of themselves that their identity seemed to depend on killing a common enemy (Girard, 1998: 105–115).

The novel as a whole reaches its climatic moment in a similar confrontation, a rally against Aboriginal land rights legislation which McIvor organises on his property. He is a much stronger character than most of them though he is also a figure of *ressentiment*. McIvor is also an embodiment of white fantasies of privilege and power which, paradoxically, arise from and often return to the feelings of disintegration and insignificance which arise from uncertainty about one's place in the scheme of things (Hage, 1998). His father was the manager of Kuran station which had belonged for generations to a rich pioneering family, heirs of privilege which he envied and aspired to. His son becomes a means to this end since he brings him up to believe that his destiny is to marry the only child of the house, a daughter. But class is an insuperable barrier and John is reminded of his social insignificance when she refuses to have anything to do with him. Humiliated, he decides to make Kuran his own one day by sheer force of determination, sacrificing everything else and alienating his wife and daughter in the process. To ensure that he keeps control even after his death, he brings John and his mother to Kuran to guarantee the succession.

In this way McIvor is a 'self made man', the type of a new society. In traditional societies, identity depends on finding one's place in it. But he makes it by an effort of will, exerting himself against his circumstances as he pursues his goal of property and power, suspicious of and hostile to anyone or anything which threatens to impede him—hence his opposition to Aboriginal land claims. The charter of the movement he founds to contest Aboriginal land rights (which, incidentally, resembles the aims of Pauline Hanson's "One Nation Party"—a political party here in Australia a few years back), reflects this ferocious and paranoid individualism and a patriotism which is largely a projection of his anxieties (which may also be true of the flag-waving rioters at Cronulla).

Those who deny the shadow side of the self imagine they actually are only what they care to know about themselves. So McIvor's patriotism rests on the conviction that his own culture and values are right and superior to all others, 'lesser breeds without the law'. Untroubled by self-reflection, he is a law unto himself (McGahan, 2004: 128). Like the early settlers he admires, might equalled right. He believes in what he calls 'the inherent value of Australian culture and traditions' which he thinks guarantee that 'the rights of the individual cannot be interfered with' (McGahan, 2004: 133). Accordingly, William, his uncle's obedient echo, responds to the challenge of Aboriginal land claims by asserting that 'Australia is our place now! You can't make us give it back!' (McGahan, 2004: 284)—assuming, incidentally, that Aborigines are not 'Australian'.

In effect, they belong to a culture which has ignored what Mircea Eliade sees as the primary task for any people settling into a country hitherto unknown to them, the 'transformation of chaos into cosmos' (Eliade, 1974: 10), a task which is essentially imaginative rather than material. Ironically McIvor's is obsessed with the land. He tells William, for instance:

> You have to know about a piece of land . . . if you're going to own it. You have to know where it fits in . . . Every stretch of land has its own story. You have to listen, and understand how it connects with other stories. Stories that involve the whole country in the end (McGahan, 2004: 106).

The view he expounds here stems from regarding the land as his own possession and a resource to be exploited. Locked in his 'closed circle around sameness' (Susin, 2002: 87) and sharing its allergy to the indefinite and inexplicable, he refuses to yield to any power other than his own. He may say that '[t]his place is alive in its own right'. But he sees that life in his own terms 'growing and changing all the time' (McGahan, 2004: 85), subjecting it to the logic of 'progress' and 'development', the logic of imperial history which, he believes, gives him his 'glorious position as basis and referent of the whole of reality spread out at [his] feet' (Susin, 2002: 80). As it drives towards the future it leaves the past behind. 'The Aborigines are gone . . . This is my property now' (McGahan, 2004: 209). They are 'not coming back' (McGahan, 2004: 100).

The novel contradicts this, however. The land has a life of its own which finally brings McIvor undone. He dies in the bushfire which destroys the house which he thinks he has made his own, consumed by the reality he has denied. So too, the rally against Aboriginal land rights which he organises with an explosion of fiery violence—the 'ethical terror' (Ricoeur, 1969: 29) which in fact underlies it—

reaches its climax. Once again fire, symbol of the sacred and of the land's power, prevails. Nor has the past been obliterated. The Aborigines have not 'died out' and the land continues to remember them. When, exploring the property, William comes upon the deep pool, once a ceremonial place, he smells 'blood and death' (McGahan, 2004: 300). The survivors of the Aboriginal people, who had been displaced by the whites, had kept coming back there. But finally the whites, determined to assert their possession, killed them and burned the bodies which they then threw into the pool to conceal what they had done. For McIvor, however, it was an important place because it was a permanent source of water. But the boy senses 'something invisible [there which] had made the air too potent to breathe ... some cold and ancient secret of the land itself' (McGahan, 2004: 326).

McGahan seems to be echoing here Judith Wright's intuition that Australian culture is like a house haunted by the 'ghost of a murdered man buried under it'. The novel's conclusion also echoes her suggestion that until it is confronted this anxiety 'would remain forever at the root of this country, making every achievement empty and every struggle vain' (Wright, 1965: 163). William's insights are important here. Until now, seduced by the prospect of inheriting Kuran and fascinated by his ferocious certainties, he has been his uncle's echo and enthralled by what holds him captive, an example of what Ricoeur calls 'the servile will' (Ricoeur, 1969: 100). He has caught occasional glimpses of a past whose 'truth was thirst and heat and twisted ghosts' and begins to realise that inheriting Kuran would be 'no gift ... [but] a burden' (McGahan, 2004: 327). Here the Aboriginal story speaks to him and, later, even more strongly, when McIvor's disaffected daughter, a lawyer and advocate of Aboriginal land rights, puts their case.

In effect he is moving out of his culture's 'closed circle around sameness', a move which marks the beginning of a genuinely ethical existence. Significantly therefore, as the novel ends, William is recovering from an operation to cure him of the ear infection he has been suffering which, also significantly, was caused by violence, by a blow from his angrily unhappy mother.

To conclude then: the connection between violence, identity and mainstream Australian culture is largely the product of what Levinas has called the 'hateful modality of the self', which has developed within this culture. But this connection can be broken by a return to what he calls a 'non-intentional consciousness', which recognises the claims of what is other-than-self, preferring 'that which justified being over that which assures it' (Hand, 1993: 85).

References

Eliade, Mircea, *The Myth Of The Eternal Return Or, Cosmos And History* (Princeton: Princeton University Press, 1974).

Girard, Rene, 'The God Of Victims', in Ward, Graham, editor, *The Postmodern God: A Theological Reader* (Oxford: Oxford University Press, 1998).

Hage, Ghassan, *White Nation: Fantasies Of White Supremacy In A Multi-Cultural Society* (Sydney: Pluto Press, 1998).

Hand, Sean, editor, *The Levinas Reader* (Oxford: Blackwell, 1993).

Ley, James, 'How Small The Lights Of Home: Andrew McGahan And The Politics Of Guilt', in *Australian Book Review*, Number 280, April 2006.

McGahan, Andrew, *The White Earth* (Sydney: Allen & Unwin, 2004).

Paul Ricoeur, *The Symbolism Of Evil* (Boston: Beacon Press, 1969).

Susin, Luiz Carlos, 'A Critique Of The Identity Paradigm', in *Cross Currents*, 55/2, Summer 2002.

Wright, Judith, *The Generations Of Men* (Melbourne: Oxford University Press, 1965).

10

'Are We Here But To Name The World?': Ways Of Naming And Praising

---

Let me take as my text some lines from the German poet Rainer Maria Rilke, lines which in effect echo one of the main themes of the Psalms, by giving voice to the praise all creation is already giving to God:

> . . . Are we, perhaps, *here*, only to say: House, Bridge. Fountain. Gate. Jug. Fruit-tree. Window. At most: Pillar. Tower . . . But to *say,* —you understand, O to *say,* with an intensity the things themselves never hoped to achieve (Rilke, 1965: 1302).

Yet the Psalms also suggest that this can be problematic. Psalm 106, for example opens with the call to 'give thanks to the Lord, for he is good; for his steadfast love endures forever'. But it follows this call with the question, 'Who can utter the mighty doings of the Lord, or declare all his praise?' The Australian Jesuit, Christopher Willcox, in a paper he gave at a conference at the monastery of New Norcia, Western Australia, quoted a sixth century Bishop, advising us to 'think of what you are singing' when we praise God in the liturgy. So let us follow this advice, asking ourselves not only what we are doing but also where and when we are doing it. The answer to the first question is that we are in a place which has been named and praised for thousands of years by the

First Peoples of this land, and that in that sense, we are carrying on that task. The answer to the second question, 'when', makes this more important. It is becoming increasingly evident in this country that particularly the earth and its creatures, ourselves included, are wounded and that this is the result of our worship of false gods. The gods are what I call the unholy trinity: Mammon, the god of money, Moloch, the god of violence and war, and McDonalds, the god of mindless and destructive pleasures.

But what difference could the liturgy, the praise of God, make? Perhaps the best response to this question is to reflect on Ludwig Wittgenstein's observation that 'the limits of my language are the limits of my world', an observation that echoes Humpty Dumpty's 'my words are the shape I am'. If, as Jean Baudrillard argues, the mass media culture in which we live 'rests on the exaltation of signs based on the denial of the reality of things' (Baudrillard, 1990: 63)—and of people—it is a culture which is essentially superficial, often deceitful (consider the way in which words like 'democracy', 'freedom' and so on are used), and out of touch with physical reality and personal experience. Taken up into 'the ecstasy of the social' (Baudrillard, 1990: 16), we are, as it were, locked out of our own hearts and left with little or no ability to speak to and of the inner depths of the self.

But that is where the God whom we believe—or better perhaps, who believes in us—speaks to us, the God Karl Rahner describes as the '"silent one" who is always there, and yet can always be overlooked [and often remains] unheard, [who] because [this reality] expresses the whole in its unity and totality, can [therefore] be passed over as meaningless' (Rahner, 1985: 46).

According to JB Metz, the best short definition of God may therefore be 'interruption' because the mystery of death and resurrection overturns what St Paul calls the 'wisdom of this world'. As Metz goes on to say, the marks of this revelation are love and solidarity, a memory which, unlike that of contemporary history, 'remembers not only what has succeeded, but also what has been destroyed, not only what has been achieved, but also what has been lost' (Metz, 1980: 171). In that way this kind of memory which we celebrate in the liturgy, is profoundly subversive since it 'works against the victory of what has become and already exists' by keeping alive the memory of those excluded from it. In our case it bears on our relations with the land's First Peoples since the resurrection is mediated by way of the memory of suffering. The dead, those already vanquished and forgotten, have a meaning which is as yet unrealised. The potential meaning of our history does not depend only on the survivors, the successful and those who make it. Meaning is not a category that is only reserved for the conquerors!

To return to the question of language, the language of the liturgy therefore should, in my opinion, challenge our present commonsense and point in the direction of realities of this kind, 'realities at present unseen'. It should take us to the depths of the self, the *cor secretum*. Poetry and music are, therefore, essential because learning about God is 'less like grasping an argument and more like understanding a musical theme', which points beyond itself to the total fabric of music (Wyschogorod, 1990: 47). Close to music as it is, this kind of language also includes gesture, the unspoken language of the body, providing a kind of echo chamber in which information gives way to intuition and a 'voice not our own', whose 'tone's deeper than intimate' may ask 'of us all we feared, yet longed to say' (Wright, 1994: 210).

In this way liturgy involves the kind of 'singing Allelulia' St Augustine writes about, that is, a richer sense of being in the world, and a larger sense of time, not a line ceaselessly moving ahead but, as the circumference of what TS Eliot calls 'the still point of the turning world', where past and future are gathered into the life of the 'Timeless One'. To refer again to the gifts traditional Aboriginal culture may have to offer, it is worth noting that it has a similar sense of time. It is something I realised when listening to a friend who had been invited to join a group of traditional people traveling out from their country not far from Alice Springs, to celebrate ceremonies with a community across the border in Wes-tern Australia. As they drove west the road gave out and, even though my friend was a good bushman, he had no idea where they were going. But his Aboriginal companions would stop, survey the country and take their bearings from a traditional song they sang about the Dreaming hero who had made the same journey when he came on earth. But this surely is what we Christians do (or should do) when we reflect on and celebrate the story of God's dealings with us, so that even as we move through time we are taking our directions from our Dreaming.

But referring to their wisdom in this way, I would argue, is not to turn away from revelation but to follow the logic of the God who can be seen, in the words of Eberhard Jüngel as 'the mystery of the world'. A God whose being, as far as we are concerned, 'is in coming' in going 'on ways to himself through this world', even if sometimes those ways seem 'to lead to other places, even to that which is not God' (Jüngel, 1983: 159). This mystery of God working in and through creation is the mystery Gerard Manley Hopkins celebrates in 'Hurrahing In Harvest', a poem in which the real harvest is the glory of God:

> I walk, I lift up, I lift up heart, eyes,

Down all that glory in the heavens to glean our Saviour . . .
And the azurous hung hills are his world-wielding shoulder
Majestic—as a stallion stalwart, very-violet-sweet
(Hopkins, 1948: 74–5).

But it is also the mystery we celebrate in the liturgy, especially when we read the Psalms, recognising the glory of God at work in the world and letting it speak through and in them and opening us out to its blessing.

This brings us finally to the eucharist, the supreme work of praise in which 'the Word' in person, 'silently, speaks and blesses, speaks to the extent that he blesses' and in which, 'eating his body and drinking his blood, [we] discover ourselves assimilated to the one whom [we] assimilate and recognise inwardly' (Marion, 1995: 151).

It is here that the synergy between 'Song, Space and Text' reaches its climax. But it is also the point at which this synergy bears most powerfully upon our world in which notions of the splendour and dignity of humanity and of creation as a whole seem to be diminishing and we are threatened with terrors created by our greed, blindness and violence, in effect by our worship of false gods. A recent essay by Denis Edwards, 'Celebrating Eucharist In A Time Of Global Climate Change' (Edwards, 2006), has some powerful things to say about the power of the eucharist and of the ways in which it may help us develop a 'cosmic theology'.

The essay begins by referring to Pope John Paul II's Encyclical, *Gift And Mystery: On The Fiftieth Anniversary Of My Priesthood* which in turn owes a great deal to Teilhard de Chardin's *The Mass On The World*. Chardin argues that in the eucharist we offer 'on the altar of the whole earth, the world's work and suffering'. This, John Paul II writes, gives us a sense of the 'universal and, so to speak, cosmic character' of the eucharist so that 'even when it is celebrated on the humble altar of a country church, [it] is always in some way celebrated *on the altar of the world'* (Edwards, 2006: 5). But uniting heaven and earth, it interrupts our history, embracing and permeating all creation with the promise of 'the Son of Man [who] became man in order to restore all creation, in one supreme act of praise, to the one who made it from nothing . . . [T]his is the *mysterium fidei* which is accomplished by the eucharist: the world which came forth from the hands of God the Creator now returns to him redeemed by Christ' (Edwards, 2006: 5).

Pope John Paul II has also written in similar vein, seeing the transubstantiated host as the 'anticipation of the transformation and divinisatiom of matter in the christological "fullness"' promised to us 'but also as providing the movement of the cosmos with its direction . . . [anticipating] its goal and at the same time [urging] it on' (Edwards, 2006: 5). This comes at a time in which the earth is being degraded and, to quote Rilke once again,

> [m]ore than ever
> the things we live with are falling away,
> are dispossessed and replaced by an act without plan
> (Rilke, 1965: 1303).

This strengthens our hope. Taking us up into the mystery of creation and redemption, it echoes the Roman Catholic Church's third eucharistic prayer's declaration that 'all creation rightly gives You praise' and intensifies its significance by joining all creation into 'cosmic companionship' with the angels and saints in their work of praise. This surely is to show us, even in these dark times, how splendid the world can be when its defeats and tragedies are taken up into the triumph of the resurrection.

As far as each of us is concerned, this gives a new intensity to the notion of the priesthood of all believers and thus new grounds of hope for and in this world. At the same time, it underlines our responsibility, the task of enabling creation to reach its fullness through us, to 'let all God's glory through' (Hopkins, 1948: 100), as it flows through our lives and worship. Rilke suggests this also in the lines with which we began since the objects he singles out for praise—house, fountain, bridge, fruit-tree and so on—are quite ordinary. Each in its own way, nurturing and expansive, make it possible for us to move on, to realise more fully our 'overflowing existence'. Nor is this merely a 'poetic' or theological conceit. Many contemporary scientists no longer see the universe as static, but as an 'energy/medium' in process of becoming (Studer, 1998: 23). They also speak increasingly, and with growing respect, of what is unseen. Some are suggesting that the cosmos is moving in the direction of increasing consciousness and that the physical universe in this way is 'both [producing] us and, ultimately [participating] *in us* to become real' (Studer, 1998: 22). Once again, this points to a connection between song, space and text, but this time the text of creation as a whole. It underlines the importance of the renewal of Christian worship and of the understanding that the world is in truth 'charged with the grandeur of God' (Hopkins, 1948: 70). Or, in Teilhard de Chardin's words, quoted by Edwards, 'the luminosity and fragrance which suffuse the universe take on the lineaments of a body and a face—Christ the Lord's' (Edwards, 2006: 6), consecrating all of creation and of humanity by taking them up into the mystery of redemption.

The liturgy in general, and the eucharist in particular, is thus the great sign of hope for our battered and suffering world and it is surely appropriate that we remember this in the weekend in which we celebrate the ascension, the conclusion of the drama of the death and resurrection of the Lord of life.

References

Baudrillard, Jean, *Revenge Of The Crystal* (Sydney: Pluto Press, 1990).

Edwards, Denis, 'Celebrating Eucharist In A Time Of Global Climate Change', in *Pacifica*, 19/1, February 2006.

Hopkins, Gerald, Manley, *Poems* (Oxford: Oxford University Press, 1948).

Jüngel, Eberhard, *God As The Mystery Of The World* (Grand Rapids: Eerdmans, 1983).

Rahner, Karl, *Foundations Of Christian Faith* (New York: Crossroad, 1985).

Rilke, Rainer, Maria *The Duinese Elegies*, 'Ninth Elegy', in Maynard Mack et al, editors, *World Masterpieces* II (New York: WW Norton, 1965).

Marion, Jean Luc, *God Without Being* (London: University of Chicago Press, 1995).

Metz, Johan Baptist *Faith In History And Society* (New York: Seabury Press, 1980).

Studer, James, 'Consciousness And Reality: Our Entry Into Creation', in *Cross Currents*, 48/1, Spring 1998.

Wright, Judith, 'Poem And Audience', in *Collected Poems: 1942–1985* (Sydney: Angus & Robertson, 1994).

Wyschogorod, Edith, *Saints And Postmodernism* (London: University of Chicago Press, 1990).

11

An Apology For The Library And For 'The Golden World Of The Imagination': A Neo-Luddite View

I begin by recalling where we are, in the first place, on land cared for and celebrated by its Aboriginal inhabitants since time immemorial and secondly on the land of the monastery of New Norcia, Western Australia, which is also hallowed, and I do this as a neo-Luddite. The original Luddites, as you know, opposed the introduction of industrial machinery, wanting to preserve the craft tradition. As Karl Marx pointed out, something was lost with the introduction of mass-production. In a way, the hand-craftsman, or woman, could be said to make him/herself in the process of working, the factory worker merely makes money. Similarly, in *Utopia*, St Thomas More, discussing the enclosures of his day as large landowners were evicting peasants to turn agricultural land into pasture for sheep—much more profitable—noted that this was a reversal of the proper order of things: once men used to eat sheep, he said, but now 'the sheep eateth up the men'.

I call myself a Luddite, though a 'neo' one, for similar reasons since I also believe in the importance of tradition (which someone has defined as 'running errands for the dead', continuing the work they began). I do not believe that everything new is automatically better than everything old nor that the primary task of libraries, for instance, is to provide information.

Central to the work of civilisation, I suggest, is the task of preserving and, if possible, expanding, that state. According to the Macquarie Dictionary 'the state of society in which a high level of art, science and government has been reached'. For a variety of reasons, this seems to be growing increasingly difficult today. But libraries are an essential resource. To put it in slogan form, they are crucial for the future as well as for the present because they preserve the past. What do I mean by that?

Most reading this, I suspect, would agree that the period of the previous Howard Government was not very inspiring. We need to ask why this was so and what that situation has asked of us. First of all I would point to the need to be realistic, not to succumb to the blandishments of a culture 'distracted by distraction from distraction' and to pretend that all has been well when clearly in so many respects this is not the case. One of Gunter Grass' novels, *The Rat*, is about this evasion. It is set in the future after civilisation has been destroyed by a nuclear holocaust. The sole survivor is a rat who looks back on the last days before this end and reflects on the gap which then existed between reality and peoples' refusal to acknowledge it as they clung to their illusions:

> Our intention was that men should learn
> little by little
> to handle not only knife and fork
> but one another as well, and reason too
> that omnipotent can opener.
>
> That once educated, the human race should freely,
> yes, freely, determine its destiny and free from its shackles
> learn to guide nature cautiously,
> as cautiously as possible,

away from chaos (Grass, 1987: 132).

A few did, it is true, begin to realise that

> something must be wrong
> I don't know what, the direction maybe.
> Some mistake, but what, has been made
> but when and where wrong,
> especially as everything's been running like clockwork,
> though in a direction
> which signs demonstrate to be wrong (Grass, 1987: 161).

But they refused to accept responsibility and to realise that

> we could all of us, just for the sake of argument, be
> the source of error, yes,
> it could be you or you or you (Grass, 1987: 161).

Maybe this is true of us today as problems environmental, social and political accumulate. But to accept this we probably need to look beyond the narrow perspectives of the present and set ourselves in the context of world history on the one hand and of the knowledge which contemporary science is providing us. We also need, I submit, to embrace notions of right and wrong beyond the self-interest fashionable today, to understand more fully what it means to be properly human and reflect not just on our rights but also on our obligations to ourselves, others and the world to which we belong. By and large, however, we have failed to do this or to recognise the crisis confronting us or to realise that, as Grass says, we may be the real source of the problem. Martin Heidegger suggested this half a century ago when he argued that the times we live in are 'destitute' 'not only because God is dead, but [because we] are hardly aware and capable of our own mortality. In effect we have not realised—or perhaps have forgotten the proper nature of our humanity, 'have not yet come into ownership of [our] own nature'. As a result 'death withdraws into the enigmatic. The mystery of pain remains veiled. Love has not been learned' (Heidegger, 1975: 96).

This is increasingly clear today. But, as Samuel Beckett remarked, 'habit is a great deadener'. We have become accustomed to the cruelties and injustices surrounding us and untroubled by them unless they affect us directly. One reason for this, I suggest, is that we have allowed others to imagine the world for us. We are gradually losing the ability to get outside our present frame of reference and see ourselves from the perspective of others and of other cultures and periods of history. This means that we have less and less sense of the possibility of ways of seeing the world and living in it and of the full range of human experience. Trapped in the 'closed circle around sameness' which the media draws around us and intent on what DH Lawrence called the 'business of money-making, money-having and money-spending', we fail to explore the mysteries of 'pain, death and love'.

But libraries do enable us to explore them, expanding our understanding of our actual experiences. They also keep us in touch with other cultures and other periods of history and thus with experiences different from our own, enabling us, as a friend of mine likes to say, to 'try on other lives for size'. Moreover they have done this over time. Monastery libraries kept European civilisation alive. It has always been one of the tasks of libraries to provide time and space for reflection in which to interrogate the reign of matter-of-fact and the direction in which the world may be heading and to do so away from the fear and suspicion which makes for the wars and rumours of wars around us. This is a crucial contribution. Kofi Annan, for instance, has warned that lack of sensitivity to other peoples' beliefs could lead to a new war of religion on a global scale. The 'golden world of the imagination', how-ever, can point us elsewhere.

As far as I know Sir Philip Sidney coined the phrase the 'golden world of the imagination', in his *Apology For Poetry*, in which he defended poetry against the literal-minded of his day—the Puritans—who regarded things imaginative with suspicion. Sidney pointed out that most other forms of knowledge have what already exists, 'the works of nature', for principal object and that they could not consist without that object. They depended on it. But that, he said, makes their inquirers 'actors and players, as it were' in preserving things as they are. 'Only the poet [by which he means the person able to create and explore possibilities yet unseen or unrealised], disdaining to be tied to any such subjection, lifted up with the vigour of his own imagination, doth grow in effect another nature, in making things either better than nature bringeth forth, or quite anew' (Abrahams, 1962: 426).

The poet Wallace Stevens who, being the well-read man that he was, had probably seen this, says something similar in his 'The Man With The Blue Guitar':

> The man bent over his blue guitar,
> A shearsman of sorts. The day was green.
>
> They said. 'You have a blue guitar,
> You do not play things as they are.'
>
> The man replied, 'Things as they are
> Are changed upon the blue guitar.'
>
> And they said then, 'But play, you must,
> A tune beyond us, yet ourselves,
>
> A tune upon the blue guitar
> Of things exactly as they are (Stevens, 1957: 52).

The discoveries of Quantum Physics point in the same direction, observing that the observer changes what is observed. Similarly writers and artists can change our perceptions of the world and thus cause us to act differently. This kind of awareness can bring about the kind of awareness and action which Gunter Grass' novel sees as so urgently necessary today as we are increasingly manipulated by images and ideas imposed on us from the outside and the inner life is neglected in the interests of conformity and fashion.

Martha Nussbaum argues that this worrying trend has other disturbing implications:

> We should regard with suspicion any claim to rule a nation of human beings by a ruler who does not acknowledge the inner moral life of each human being, its strivings and complexities, its complicated emotions, its efforts at understanding and its terrors, [and which] does not distinguish in its descriptions between a human being and a machine (Nussbaum, 1995: 38).

Emmanuel Levinas expanded on this when he wrote that 'it is in the laying down by the ego of its sovereignty . . . that we find ethics and also very probably the very spirituality of the soul, but most certainly the question of the meaning of being' (Hand, 1993: 85)—something which most of the world's religious traditions have always known.

But 'the meaning of being' is not at the centre of public discussion today. Instead the centre seems to be the will of 'the Market' and the state of the economy. But the tradition preserved in libraries makes it clear that there are 'more things in heaven and earth than are dreamed of' by *homo economicus,* more expansive, life-giving and creative realities. As Erasmus remarked, 'man is not born man but becomes man'. Every technological advance or historical development therefore calls us to redefine and expand our notions of our humanity.

Books which help us to think and feel with, for and through the lives of others obviously have an important part to play in this process. As William Blake pointed out, in an important sense ultimately the world is neither round nor flat but human-shaped: the way things are reflects our values and our notions of reality—and the contemporary understanding of the power of ideology confirms this. It is becoming increasingly clear, for example, that a world addicted to the worship of what I call the 'Unholy Trinity, Mammon (the god of money), Moloch (the god of violence and competition) and McDonald's (the god of destructive pleasures) threatens our existence as human beings along with the world in which we live and on which we depend.

This throws further light not only on Heidegger's proposition that we live in a 'destitute time' but also on his point that hope remains because 'song (that is, the kind of imaginative thinking and feeling we are talking about) remains': 'the singers still keep to the trace of the holy' (Heidegger, 1975: 97). This brings us to the point where he begins, which we did not consider earlier: that our time is destitute because 'God is dead'—Nietzsche's proposition, of course. Heidegger cancels this out, however, when he argues that the 'singers' refuse to accept this and 'keep to the trace of the holy.' Paul Ricoeur's discussion of the idea that 'God is dead' illuminates what Heidegger is getting at. But it also strengthens the argument for the importance of libraries.

According to Ricoeur 'the true question is to know, first of all, which god is dead; then, who has killed him (if it is true that this death is a murder); and finally, what sort of authority belongs to the announcement of this death' (Ricoeur, 1974: 445). The god who is dead, he suggests, is an abstraction, the 'First Cause', omnipotent, omniscient and so on and 'out there' who is ultimately perhaps, as Marx argued, merely a human projection of emotional, social, political or economic need. His death was in effect a suicide since this was no god in the proper sense of the word; that is, this was not a reality beyond human comprehension. So the authority which belongs to the announcement of this death is that of a Living God whose 'being is in coming' who 'goes on ways to himself' through this world in our human experience and in the community of belief, even when [these ways] lead to other places, even to that which is not God' (Jüngel, 1983: 159), opening up new possibilities for our humanity and for our understanding of the 'privilege and panic' of our mortality and of the mysteries of pain, death and love.

So Martha Nussbaum, to quote her again, can argue:

> A life which is properly human involves a going beyond the facts, an acceptance of generous fancies, a projection of our sentiments and inner activities on the forms we perceive about us (and a recognition from this interaction of images of ourselves, of our own inner world) . . . We are all of us, insofar as we interact morally and politically, fanciful projectors, makers and believers in fictions and metaphors (Nussbaum, 1995: 24).

Evidently, this brings us back again to the library, where as Milton described it:

> there be pens and heads . . . sitting by their studious lamps, musing, searching, revolving new notions and ideas wherewith to present, as with their homage and fealty, the approaching

Reformation: others as fast reading, trying all things, assenting to the force of reason and convincement. For him the library was a place of creativity in which people could pursue 'the light which . . . was given to us, not to be ever staring on, but by it to discover onward things more remote from our knowledge (Milton, 1962: 908–10).

It is true, of course, that it can be dangerous to organise our lives entirely from books. Ideologues like Hitler and Stalin, not to mention the neo-Cons of our day and Grand Inquisitors of all kinds in the past and present, have done so with destructive consequences for human dignity and integrity. But, as Milton suggests, books which provoke new kinds of understanding as well as information can open up creative gaps and fissures in our present certainties, raise doubts and questions about them and keep alive the hope. Books are 'the long-distance runner', as Gunter Grass calls it, of new and richer possibilities, calling us to continue the search for 'the meaning behind the meaning' of things, asking us even in the darkest of times not to put our trust in the way things are at the moment. So the story goes that when Vita Sackville-West was asked whether she wrote about the 'real world' she replied: 'Certainly not. One of the damn things is quite enough'. At the same time we must also hope that things as they are can be 'changed upon the blue guitar' of the imagination.

But this is not, and should not be, always a serious business. The 'golden world of the imagination' can also be playful and offer a lively and compassionate insight into the oddities of human beings, the pathos as well as the strangeness of our eccentricities. Let me give you an example. Amos Oz is an Israeli writer of some note whose autobiography tells of his growing up as the only child of

Jewish migrants. They arrived with little money from Poland where the family had once been well-to-do, into an Israel still under British rule. It was not an easy life, especially as his parents' marriage seems to have been pretty loveless. But Oz rejoices in the ways in which, despite everything, people managed to preserve their dignity. One of my favourite passages is his story of his Auntie Greta, who loved going shopping and trying on clothes she could never afford to buy. His account is full of the small boy's wonder at her daring and his own anxieties: Auntie Greta would drag me into three or four clothes shops, in each of which she liked to try on, take off, and try on again, in the privacy of the changing cubicle, a number of beautiful dresses and a range of magnificent skits, blouses and nightdresses, and a mass of colourful house coats that she termed negligees. Once she even tried on a fur: the look in the tortured eyes of the slain fox terrified me. The fox's face stirred my soul because it looked both cunning and heart-wrenchingly wretched. But there is also a half-understood and realised compassion for her: Time and again this broad-beamed Aphrodite was reborn from the foam, bursting from behind the curtain in a new and ever more glamorous incarnation. For my benefit and for the salesperson and other shoppers she would turn on her heel a couple of times in front of the mirror. Despite her heavy thighs she enjoyed executing a coquettish pirouette, and enquired of each of us in turn whether it suited her, whether it flattered her, whether it clashed with the colour of her eyes, whether it hung well, didn't it make her look fat, wasn't it rather common, a bit brash? As she did so, her face reddened, and because she was embarrassed at blushing she blushed again, that deeper blood-red, verging on purple. Finally she promised the salesperson earnestly that she would almost certainly be back the same day, in fact very shortly, after lunch, by the end of the afternoon, when she'd had time just to look around some other shops, tomorrow at the latest.

So far as I can recall she never ever went back. On the contrary she was always very careful never to visit the same shop twice until several months had elapsed (Oz, 2005: 214).

Passages like this surely justify Sidney's saying that the 'poet' can have a priestly function. So Oz celebrates here his aunt's confused longings for beauty and admiration, giving us a sense of wonder and awe before the possibilities of otherwise undistinguished people.

It is time to conclude. So let us return to the idea that our present culture appears to be moving in the wrong direction and that we are losing any real sense of responsibility for it. What I have been arguing, however, is that a central task of the library is to empower the 'golden world of the imagination', to enable us to recover a sense of the wonder and awe at the possibilities implicit even in the most ordinary existence, to break out of the closed circle of one-dimensional materialism with the ability

> To see a world in a Grain of Sand,
> And a heaven in a wild flower,
> Hold Infinity in the palm of your hand
> And Eternity in an hour.

In turn this may lead us to an understanding of the ways in which our perceptions may shape the world and of our responsibilities for it, realising that, as Blake said,

> The bat that flits at close of eve
> Has left the brain that won't believe
> and that
> The dog starv'd at his master's gate
> Predicts the ruin of the state (Blake, 1961: 118).

It may be true that, as most of our literal-minded leaders and opinion-makers would say, writing of this imaginative kind may 'make nothing happen'. Yet, in his elegy for the poet WB Yeats, Auden, conceding this, goes on to affirm its continuing power, that

> . . . it survives
> In the valley of its saying where executives
> Would never want to tamper . . .
> A way of happening, a mouth (Auden: 1962, 1626).

References

Abrams, MH, *et al*, editors, *The Norton Anthology Of English Literature* I. (New York: WW Norton, 1962).

Auden, WH, 'In Memory Of WB Yeats', in David Daiches, *et al* editors, *The Norton Anthology Of English Literature* II (New York: WW Norton, 1962).

Blake, William, 'Auguries Of Innocence', in *William Blake: Complete Poetry And Prose*, edited by Geoffrey Keynes (London: Nonesuch Press, 1961).

Grass, Gunter, *The Rat*, translated by Ralph Mannheim (London: Secker and Warburg 1987).

Hand, Sean, editor, *The Levinas Reader* (Oxford: Blackwell, 1993).

Heidegger, Martin, *Poetry, Language, Thought* (New York: Colophon Books, 1975).

Jüngel, Eberhard, *God As The Mystery Of The World* (Grand Rapids: Eerdmans, 1983).

Milton, John *Areopagiica*, in Abrams, MH, *et al*, editors, *The Norton Anthology Of English Literature* I. (New York: WW Norton, 1962).

Nussbaum, Martha, *Poetic Justice: The literary Imagination And Political Life* (Boston: Beacon Books, 1995).

Oz, Amos *A Tale Of Love And Darkness* (London: Vintage, 2005).

Ricoeur, Paul, *The Conflict Of Interpretations*, edited by Don Idhe (Evanston: Northwestern University Press, 1974).

Stevens, Wallace, *Selected Poems* (London: Faber & Faber, 1957).

12

'What Is Truth?', Said Jesting Pilate, And Did Not Stay To Hear

---

This is the opening of Sir Francis Bacon's essay 'On Truth' written in the sixteenth century. I don't want to pursue Bacon's further argument here. What I want to do, however, is to reflect on the fact that many of our contemporaries today would share his scepticism. As Jean Baudrillard suggests, in a culture which rests on 'the exaltation of signs based on the denial of the reality of things' (Baudrillard, 1990: 63)—and, I would add of people—everything is oversignified. So meaning —which I'm assuming at the moment is another word for 'truth'—seems not only undesirable but also unattainable. In that sense most of us are like Pilate, have little sense of any authority, any over-riding order outside the self and therefore tend to 'bow down in *amor fati* (love of fate) . . . before the powers that be', as Adorno puts it and attribute 'reality to wishes and meaning to senseless compulsion' (Adorno, 1994: 98). At the other extreme, fundamentalists of all kinds, religious, political and economic, claim that they and they alone know the 'truth' and that they and they alone possess it.

What then is my take on this situation? Here again I find Bacon helpful because he was referring to *John* 18: 38, the scene in which Jesus stands before the Roman governor who asks him 'What is truth?' As Bacon says, Pilate does not stay to hear any answer that might be given. But, had he been among the disciples earlier that night, he would have heard Jesus declare: 'I am the way, and the truth, and the life' (*John*, 14: 5). We do not know what Bacon would have made of this: probably nothing much because his priorities were political—our old friend 'law and order'.

Theology, I know, is academically unfashionable at the moment. Nevertheless I believe it is the case, as William James argued, that religious experiences 'have the right to be absolutely authoritative over the individuals to whom they come' (Rashkova, 2006: 150). So it may be that they may provide a point of reference if we are to find a way of coping with the clash between conflicting notions of truth, that is, of reality and value.

The words attributed to Jesus here, after all, suggest that 'truth' is not something abstract and propositional but experiential, and a revelation—a suggestion here of the Greek notion of *alêtheia?*—of him and the way he lives. But it is a way which points beyond itself to a reason and order beyond our comprehension and control, the mystery of what is ultimately the case to which he was attuned and to which he was obedient. (According to some Scripture scholars, the 'I am' sayings in *John* make this claim.)

This is not to say, as fundamentalists do, that Scripture sets out a clear map of reality and code of behaviour. To the contrary, the 'truth' embodied in Jesus has to be experienced and lived out by each person according to her/his lights in her/his particular context who is attempting, as St Thomas More was supposed to have said, to 'serve God wittily in the tangle of our mind'. Conscience in that sense—as Christian tradition has held almost universally—is therefore the ultimate authority. True, as Walter Benjamin noted, in a culture which 'rests on the exaltation of signs at the expense of the reality of things and people', experience has fallen in value and it looks as if it has fallen into bottomlessness' (Weigl, 2006: 26), with the result that, paradoxically, the word 'truth' has often become a weapon against others and a means of self-justification.

Examples abound in the 'war on terror', American policy in the Middle East and so on. But I propose an example closer to home: the relations between Aboriginal and non-Aboriginal Australians. Essentially there is a clash here of notions of 'truth', of conflicting notions of reality and value, though of the two it seems to me that ours is the more intransigent and determined that our 'truth', our way of living in the world, must prevail. That is perhaps because colonizing cultures tend to be dogmatic, sure that we have the truth and represent the growing point of civilisation. So we regard ourselves as the centre of understanding, especially of ethical understanding, 'distinguishing and identifying good and evil in a particular way based on [ourselves], on [our] glorious position as basis and referent of the whole of reality spread out at [our] feet' (Susin, 2000; 80). 'White' thus becomes synonymous with 'civilised' and 'responsible' and 'black' with 'savage' and 'irresponsible'. In effect, even those who wish Aboriginal people well, tended to believe that the best thing is to assimilate them to our culture.

This, however, is a form of arrogance. The fact is that 'truth' has an ethical dimension since it involves respect for the views of others and the realities of the world around us as well as a sense of responsibility for and to the other. Faced with the interrogation of our right to be who we are and live as we wish to do in a new situation, in a strange new place and confronted by people very different from ourselves, as we were, we appealed to the absolute and anonymous law of imperial certainty, failing to recognise the rights and way of life of the others who had lived here so long before us. In that sense the truth we asserted had little valency since one of its mark is to interrogate convention and habit in the name of a larger understanding, some 'reality which is not yet real', beyond the logic of history where might often equals right. Truth submits that there may be a wisdom different in kind from the one we value—at least if we define wisdom as its etymology suggests we should: *Wys* is the Anglo-Saxon equivalent of the Greek *arête*, the perfection of a person or thing, and *dom* is a suffix which signifies an abiding state, so that wisdom properly describes a person attuned to what is ultimately the case. If this is so, then truth may help situate us in a larger scheme of things and we non-Aboriginal Australians may have things to learn from Aboriginal culture.

But the notion of 'truth' we are proposing may interrogate the logic of our culture in another way. According to JB Metz, the best definition of this truth is 'interruption' (Metz, 1980: 171). But the neo-Darwinian premises on which we operate assumes that the 'winners' represent the growing point of history and that the 'losers' deserve to be subordinate to and obey them, if they are not to disappear from the stage of history. I would argue, however, that a richer and fuller conception of the world interrupts this belief, suggesting that 'losers' may have a meaning yet to be realised, that 'the history of human suffering is not merely part of the pre-history of freedom but remains an inner aspect of *the* history of freedom'. So JB Metz argues that 'freedom degenerates wherever those who suffer are treated more or less as a cliché and degraded to a faceless mass' (Metz, 1980: 112–3). This, I suggest, is a truth we need to preserve and so enlarge this kind of freedom.

So it may be that the notions of reality and value by which our present culture lives is at odds with the truth, at least if we accept Socrates' point that the more we know the more we know we do not know and need to know. Let me conclude then with another theological reference. The story of Pentecost can be seen as concluding the story of the 'way, truth and life' since it opens into a future. It implies that 'the reconciliation of the tensions and conflicts that come with plurality does not lie in returning to [a] lost unity' but that 'we should speak in such a way that everyone hears the truth in their own language' (Borgman 2006: 141).

References

Adorno, Theodor, *Minima Moralia* (London: Verso, 1994).

Baudrillard, Jean, *Revenge Of The Crystal: Selected Writings On The Modern Object And Its Destiny* (Sydney: Pluto Press, 1990).

Borgman Erik, 'Theology: Discipline At The Limits', in *Concilium*, 55/2, Summer 2006.

Kaufmann, David, 'Adorno: In Light of "The Light of Transcendence": Redemption in Adorno', in Cristaudo, Wayne & Baker, Wendy, editors, *Messianism Apocalypse & Redemption In Twentieth Century German Thought* (Adelaide: ATF Press, 2006).

Hand, Sean, editor, *The Levinas Reader* (Oxford: Blackwell, 1993).

Metz, Johan Baptist, *Faith In History And Sociey* (New York: Seabury Press, 1980).

Rashkova, Randi, 'Religion And The University', in *Cross Currents*, 55/2, Summer 2006.

Susin, Luiz Carlos, 'A Critique Of The Identity Paradigm, in *Concilium*, 51/2, Summer 2002

Turner, Ian, editor, *The Australian Dream* (Melbourne: 1968.

Weigl, Engelhard, 'Theodicy Between Messianism and Apocalypse in German Philosophy', in Cristaudo, Wayne & Baker, Wendy, editors, *Messianism Apocalypse & Redemption In Twentieth Century German Thought* (Adelaide: ATF Press, 2006).

13

'Such Is Life My Fellow Mummers': The Seditious Joseph Furphy

---

Words, as Joseph Furphy has Tom Collins say, are tricky things, as slippery as wet melon seeds when you try to pick them up. So the current attempts to define 'Australian values' tend to be rather bemusing and in the long run lead me at least to conclude that the phrase, like the word beauty, points to something which largely exists in the eye of the beholder. Unfortunately that does not prevent them being used, especially by politicians, to paint those who disagree with them as suspect, even guilty of sedition. Sedition, though, is a word which has a fairly clear meaning, probably because it has legal and political origins, being defined as incitement of discontent or rebellion against government.

But those origins go back to the days of absolute monarchy and to rulers intent on preserving absolute power. Most of us would like to think, however, that this is not the kind of government we have today, that we live in a democracy. This is an even more slippery word, of course, but one that implies diversity and debate as people work at building community together under the umbrella of a set of values which includes respect for individuals and for their beliefs and opinions and for the right to dissent and ask questions about the decisions of power. To come to the question at issue—sedition. If questioning the status quo and being in disagreement with certain governmental policies is seen as seditious then that in fact can be seen as an important element in the history of 'Australian values' and the current trend to use the term 'un-Australian' to enforce conformity is dangerously totalitarian in its implications.

In my more optimistic moments, however, I like to think that this kind of behaviour is not because government has totalitarian tendencies. Rather, its leaders have little sense of history, of the real—as distinct from romanticised—story of ordinary people, those former Prime Minister John Howard liked to call the 'battlers', and even less sense of the First Peoples who have lived here from time immemorial. Instead, they live in the instantaneous present addicted to what DH Lawrence called the 'business of money-making, money-having and money-spending, bemused by fantasies of endless material expansion and consumption'. The reality of the past is 'another country' so that those who believe we may have something to learn from it are suspect.

Exploring it, however, may contribute to the current discussion of 'Australian values' and help us understand better what the phrase implies. One way of doing this is by looking at imaginative evidence from the past since it can give a sense of the ways in which we have come to understand ourselves and our place in the world. One such piece of evidence is one which the literal minded and those with no time for jokes—the majority, I suspect, of those in positions of power—would probably regard as profoundly seditious and probably frivolous. Its author described it as not just 'a collection of lies, but one long involved lie, in 7 chapters' (Cathels, 1981: 419) and boasted of its 'outspoken contempt of fetish . . . calm Australian sufficiency, and . . . disregard of hostile opinion' (Furphy, 1981: 406) as it pursues its self-ironic way. That work is Joseph Furphy's *Such Is Life*, one of the seminal texts of what used to be called 'the Australian tradition'.

Its opening sentence, 'Unemployed at last!' (Furphy, 1981: 3) should upset those concerned to deal severely with 'dole bludgers' and 'welfare cheats'—though in defence of the offender, Furphy's narrator Tom Collins, it has to be said that he did then begin to write a book. Nevertheless there is no sense that work is the basis of citizenship and the only proper occupation for human beings: his characters spend most of their time talking, yarning to one another about the meaning of life in general and stories of good and bad luck in particular. It also mocks the narrow pragmatic and utilitarian premises of our culture, proclaiming in pseudo-heroic mode that Tom's unemployment is not the result of social but of cosmic causes: 'the momentum of Original Impress has been tending towards this far-off, divine event ever since a scrap of fire-mist flew from the solar centre to form our planet' (Furphy, 1981: 1).

Equally seditious to people who supported the former government line, is the fact that its characters are mostly people 'of no fixed address', bullock drivers (who in the days before the coming of the railways provided transport for settlers in the outback, carting supplies to them and bringing their wool back on the return trip) and drovers, people who existed on the fringes of society and had scant respect for establishment manners, values and pieties. They would not, I suspect, have been impressed by the invocation of 'Australian values' for political purposes, being far too busy learning to deal with the realities confronting ordinary people on the frontier. One of them, the bullock driver 'Mosey' Price, for instance, mocks the myth of Burke and Wills, dismissing Wills as a 'pore harmless weed' but attacking Burke for his aristocratic pretensions—'Don't sicken a man with yer Burke. He burked that expegition, right enough. "Howlt! Dis-MOUNT!" Grand style o' man for sich a contract! I tell you, that (explorer) died for want of sherry an' biscakes'

—and for his incompetent bush-craft, declaring that 'there ain't a drover, nor yet a bullock driver, nor yet a stockkeeper, from 'ere to 'ell that couldn't a bossed that expegition straight through to the Gulf, an' back agen, an' never turned a hair—with sich a season as Burke had' (Furphy, 1981: 26).

Burke relied on his image as a 'gentleman'. But for Alf images counted for nothing. What mattered was to confront a difficult environment relying on courage, commonsense and the help of others simply doing their job. His attack on the myth is based on his respect for these people and their achievements and he spoke with the authority of experience, having travelled through that country himself and knowing that his father had passed by Burke's camp and been scandalised by all the 'paravinalia' he had which even included a cupboard designed to fit on one of the camels 'for his swell toggery, an' . . . one o' the compartments made to hold his belltopper' (Furphy, 1981: 27) Evidently his attitude to the present culture which, according to Jean Baudrillard, 'rests on the exaltation of signs based on the denial of the reality of things' (Baudrillard, 1990: 63), would be profoundly subversive. He would have agreed with the epigraph to *Tristram Shandy,* a book similarly fascinated with the uses of social signals and a book which Furphy also admired, that 'it is not things that upset men but their judgments about things'.

Not surprisingly then Furphy had little time for empire in general and for the British Empire in particular, believing that they had no respect for the individual but were 'committed to . . . usages of petrified injustice . . . clogged by . . . fealty to shadowy idols, enshrined by Ignorance, and upheld by misplaced homage alone' (Furphy, 1981: 66). His hope, however, was that Australia might become a different kind of society whose temper, as he said of his book, would be 'democratic' and its bias 'offensively Australian'. So it is not difficult to imagine what he would think of a prime minister who celebrated the centenary of the Australian nation with a visit to London and glories in his friendship with the US President.

Nevertheless, Furphy's nationalism is relatively subtle; it is not so much, as someone has said, a matter of 'what a gum tree looks but what a gum tree means'. What it meant for him had to do with the interplay between self and the environment as well as self and others. So he had no desire to recreate 'a new Britannia in another world' as many of the more privileged settlers wanted to do. He acknowledged the sheer difference of the place from anything on the other side of the world. As he saw it, the environment was one which cut human pretentiousness down to size: 'We are all walking along the shelving edge of a precipice; any one of us may go at any moment, or be dragged down by another' (Furphy, 1981: 94). There is nothing here of our current overweening confidence in technology and the Global Economy. The book's opening scene sets the tone, reminding me of Pascal's description of the infinity of space and our finitude, showing Tom making his way across the Riverina plain under the 'geodosic curve' of the sky as 'the dark boundary of the scrub country disappears northward in the glassy haze, and, in front, southward, the level black plains of Riverina Proper mark a straight sky-line' (Furphy, 1981: 4).

It is true that one could link this with 'the vision splendid/Of the sunlit plains extended' which underpins the colonial myth of 'development'. But, as Paul Carter points out, that is a myth in which 'Nature's painted curtains are drawn aside to reveal heroic man at his heroic labour on the stage of history' (Carter, 1987: xv). But Furphy's view of our place in the scheme of things is anything but heroic. He attacks the Burke and Wills expedition, for example, because heroic pretension prevailed over understanding of the land and respect for its power and attempted. His contempt for its failure to take land's power into account and attempting instead to impose their ways on it—in contrast with bullockies like Mosey Alf who had learned to respect it, knowing that, if they did not, the country itself would 'pretty quickly fetch [them] to [their] proper level' (Furphy, 1981: 26).

There are many examples of this: the swagman who dies of thirst, exhaustion and 'the final collapse of hope' (Furphy, 1981: 80) in sight of Rory O'Halloran's hut, of Rory's daughter
who wanders away from home, loses her way and dies in the bush, of settlers driven off the land by droughts and floods as well by the 'dirty tricks' of people richer and more powerful than they. As O'Halloran puts it, looking down on the dead body of the swagman and reflecting on the land's 'levelling power: '"We're poor helpless craythurs Tammas"' (Furphy, 1981: 80). All of this questions the arrogance of devotees of 'development' and technology today and their remarkable indifference to danger signs in the world around us.

Essentially, then, Furphy is sceptical of power unless it took account of this kind of physical reality and preferred the needs of the powerless to the powerful. As a representative figure Tom is therefore a self-ironic figure, describing himself as having been a government official, of the ninth class 'paid rather according to my grade than my merit, and not in proportion to the loafing I had to do' (Furphy, 1981: 4). His experience of the outback is the main source of this scepticism. Position and wealth count for little here where droughts, floods and fires on the one hand and booms and bust in the economy mean that there existed even few rich men who could not imagine a combination of circumstances that would have given [them] lodgings under the bridge?—that may still do so, say, within twelve months?' (Barnes, 1981: 94).

The figure of Willoughby, an English gentleman down on his luck, exemplifies this precariousness. His education and sense of social superiority have rendered him unable to adapt to a situation in which 'urbane address, faultless syntax . . . [and] the calm consciousness of inherent superiority, are of little use'. Tom sees him as a 'poor shadow of departed exclusiveness as he sits among the bullock drivers around the campfire dependent on their help and hospitality and reflects that 'without doubt it is easier to acquire gentlemanly deportment than axe-man's muscle' (Furphy, 1981: 32) but that in the situation in which they find themselves the latter is essential and the former largely irrelevant.

Obviously this interrogates a culture in which, as Marshall McLuhan put it, it is necessary to 'love one's label as oneself'. But it could be argued that even, or perhaps especially in it, the meaning of human worth which preoccupied Furphy and others like him may still demand consideration. For one thing, today, physical reality is beginning to reassert its claims in the environmental crisis confronting us. For another, it could be argued that rule by rhetoric, by words with little foundation in fact, undermines the social fabric since as a form of dishonesty it damages trust and understanding. Furphy understood this, as one occasion in which Tom uses this tactic suggests—admittedly in a good cause, trying to persuade the unsympathetic boundary rider Sollicker to return to a sick bullocky the bullocks he confiscated from him while he was lying incapacitated in his camp.

Visiting Sollicker at home and noticing his small son, Tom tries to flatter him, invoking the idea then fashionable of the 'Coming Australian', and tells him that the boy is one of 'a race of people . . . such as the world has never seen before' (Furphy, 1981: 143). But the strategy fails and Tom reflects that 'nothing is easier than to build Nankin palaces of porcelain theory, which will fall in splinters before the first canon shot of unparleying fact'. He had no authority to 'dogmatise about the 'Coming Australian'—a version in his day of our talk about 'Australian values' —and that in fact this kind of talk 'is a problem' and concluding that 'deductive reasoning of this [sloganising] kind is seldom safe' (Furphy, 1981: 144).

The 'unparleying fact' he relied on was of the physical, social and economic reality which confronted the people he described attempting to make their way in a difficult environment. He was contemptuous of those who would romanticise the situation. He particularly despised 'novels of the *Geoffrey Hamlyn* class . . . [like] Henry Kingsley's exceedingly trashy and misleading novel' which was peopled, he thought, with 'slender-witted, virgin-souled, overgrown schoolboys' (Furphy, 1981: 164), totally unfitted to life on the frontier, contrasting them with writers like Zola: 'He is honest; he never calls evil, good' (Furphy, 1981: 245). So one can imagine what Furphy would have to say about contemporary advertising, the masters of spin who guide our rulers and manage much of our media.

For him the foundation of life in society was ethical, the well-being of every person, regardless of social position and wealth. So he was profoundly critical of the society around him which failed to ensure this for the powerless men and women who people his book for whom mere survival often involved a series of 'dirty transactions' (Furphy, 1981: 12). One of the bullockies makes this point in an early scene which describes them preparing to let their bullocks on to station land to graze for the night. This was illegal since it involved 'stealing' the grass which 'belonged' to the station owner. So Tom, the former bureaucrat remarks that 'this would appear a dirty transaction'. To which one of them, Thompson, replies: '"If you want a problem to work out, just consider that

God constructed cattle for living on grass, and the grass to live on, and that, last night, and tonight, and tomorrow night, and mostly every night, we've a choice between two dirty transactions—one is, to let the bullocks starve, and the other is to steal grass for them"' (Furphy, 1981: 12).

Furphy's comment on this dilemma is to conclude the scene by returning to the cosmic perspective with which *Such Is Life* begins, signalling a tension between the law of society and a more universal sense of right and wrong,—a tension which still exists today, especially in matters of public policy, even if it is seldom referred to. So Thompson describes the injustice of his situation: '"I'm sick and tired of studying why some people should be in a position where they have to go out of their way to do wrong, and other people are cornered to the extent that they can't live without doing wrong"' (Furphy, 1981: 12). But then the narrative pits beyond this situation, seditiously drawing attention to the much larger order of reality: 'It was a clear but moonless night; the dark blue canopy spangled with myriad stars—grandeur, peace and purity above; squalor, worry, and profanity below. Fit basis for many an ancient system of theology—unscientific, if you will, but by no means contemptible' (Furphy, 1981: 13).

It is by opening up this perspective, I suggest, that Furphy is most subversive since it points to the need to redefine current one-dimensional notions of reality and value. In this long perspective, money and social position are of little account. So it is possible for one of his characters to declare: '"We draw no colour line, no educational line, not even an intellectual line, but we fix a very distinct standard of progress potential"' (Furphy, 1981: 33)—which in this context would mean the obligation to ensure that each person is able to achieve dignity and satisfaction. Tom points to this obligation on another occasion, for example, when he remarks: 'Heaven knows I am no more inclined to decry social culture than moral principle; but I acknowledge no aristocracy except one of service and self-sacrifice in which he that is chief shall be servant of all, and he that is greatest of all, servant of all' (Furphy, 1981: 33).

This sense of obligation to the other is not fashionable now, and it certainly subverts the way competition tends to prevail over cooperation, installing the supremacy of might over right. So Furphy suspects the value placed on 'success', usually defined in economic terms, being aware of its human cost, and thus interrogates the narrative of 'progress', describing the 'successful pioneer', for example, as 'the early bird' and the 'forgotten pioneer' as 'the early worm'. The former 'is the man who never spared others; [the latter] the man who never spared himself, but, being a fool, built houses for wise men to live in, and omitted to gather moss', making a Raleigh-cloak of himself to afford free and pleasant passage for the noblest work of God, namely, the Business Man' (Furphy, 1981: 86). This could surely be seen by many today as blasphemy indeed.

But this, to refer belatedly to it, is the reason for the disjunctive nature of his narrative which reflects his ironic sense of reality and of our ambiguous place in it. It contrasts markedly with the self-confident belief that human beings are in charge of the universe, a belief which, despite all the evidence to the contrary, underpins our culture. As one critic points out *a propos* Pascal's fragmentary way of setting out his philosophy, disjuncture may be the best way to break out of a monolithic world view into a larger sense of reality:

> Pascal's message is that Man [sic] is great in that he searches for absolute values but small in that, without ever ceasing to search, he knows that he can never approach these values. The only form to express this context is . . . one which does not prove the contrary; which does not show either [someone] who has abandoned the search or one

who has approached the goal. The fragment is
such a form (Goldmann, 1955: 37).

Furphy, too, a postmodernist before his time, rejects grand narratives to focus on the task of living in a complex and challenging universe, refusing to accept an identity imposed from outside by society, affirming his own responsibility and the risky ambiguities of his situation. But this, paradoxically, is what makes his world view so cheerfully creative—in contrast with the anxieties underneath the surface of the apparent self-confidence of Western culture today. It is creative because, as Martha Nussbaum argues:

> A life which is properly human involves a going beyond the facts, an acceptance of generous fancies, a projection of our sentiments and inner activities on the forms we perceive about us (and a recognition from this interaction of ourselves, our inner world) . . . We are all of us, insofar as we interact morally and politically, fanciful projectors, makers and believers in fictions and metaphors (Nussbaum, 1995: 24).

Put another way, the sense of vast unconsciousness of nature which pervades Furphy's work leads ultimately to the agnostic sense of the vast nature of consciousness with which *Such Is Life* concludes:

> Such is life, my fellow mummers—just like a poor player, that bluffs and feints his hour upon the stage, and then cheapens down to mere nonentity. But let me not hear any small witticism to the further effect that its story is a tale told by avulgarian, full of slang and blanky, signifying—nothing (Barnes, 1981: 297).

If this is subversive, this kind of subversion may be badly needed today.

References

Baudrillard, Jean, *Revenge Of The Crystal* (Sydney: Pluto Press, 1990).

Carter, Paul, *The Road To Botany Bay* (London: Faber & Faber, 1987).

Furphy, Joseph, 'Letter to William Cathels' in Barnes, John, editor, *Portable Australian Author: Joseph Furphy* (St Lucia: University of Queensland Press, 1981).

Furphy, Joseph, review of *Such Is Life,* in Barnes, John, editor, *Portable Australian Author: Joseph Furphy* (St Lucia: University of Queensland Press, 1981).

Goldmann, William, *Le Dieu Cache* (Paris: Gallimard, 1955).

Nussbaum, Martha, *Poetic Justice: The Literary Imagination And Political Life* (Boston: Beacon Press, 1995).